KABDWAL BOOK INTERNATIONAL (KBI Publishers) was established on 28th February' 2003 by Naveen Chand Kabdwal. Our journey began by marketing traditional technical and management books. In 7 years of working, we realized the need for International Standards. Result of this need, KABDWAL BOOK INTERNATIONAL entered in the field of foreign standards.

With our continuous efforts of pursuing the needs of International Standards, fair and smooth dealing, most of the international agencies gave us the opportunity to deal directly for their published standards.

In 2014 we published our first book and after a hiatus of 8 years we resumed our journey in publishing.

Words of Praise

"Strategic Business Communication is a game-changer for professionals looking to turn language into leadership. With practical strategies and real-world insights, it equips readers to communicate with clarity, confidence, and cultural intelligence. A must-read for those seeking to master business English and amplify their executive presence. Kudos to Preeti for this invaluable guide to strategic communication!"

— **Group Captain Sandip Sarkar**,
Purpose & Leadership Coach (ICF- PCC)
LinkedIn Top Voice

"This book is a must-have toolkit for professionals seeking to master business communication. Preeti combines NLP and Executive Presence expertise to address challenges, provide actionable solutions, and refine business English. A powerful guide to overcoming barriers and elevating leadership impact."

— **Sanjeeb Lahiri**,
Chief HR Officer, GRP Ltd.
Top 100 Great People Manager-India 2023

"Strategic Business Communication" is a well-structured and insightful guide that bridges the gap between theory and real-world application. She shares practical strategies and tools that enhances workplace communication. The book offers clear frameworks and engaging examples, simplifying complex concepts while emphasizing their strategic importance. A must-read for anyone looking to refine their business communication skills, drive impactful interactions and achieve measurable business results."

— **Mangesh Wagle**
Carnegie Master and Associate Vice President-Training,
Dale Carnegie India

"This book is a masterclass in effective communication, offering actionable insights and practical strategies for business success. With its engaging tone and real-world examples, this book is a must-read for professionals, entrepreneurs, and students seeking to enhance their communication skills. Preeti's expertise shines through, making this book an invaluable resource for anyone looking to communicate with clarity, confidence, and impact."

— **Renu Gupta**,
Director-Quality Assurance and Regulatory Affairs-Japan
and Asia Pacific, Beckman Coulter Diagnostics

"Your book on Strategic Business Communication is an invaluable resource for professionals looking to enhance their communication skills. Practical, insightful, and impactful, it makes a significant contribution to the field."

— **Samar Mahapatra**,
Principal HR Consultant, HR India
Amongst India's Top 50 CHROs

"Strategic Business Communication is a well-structured and logically sequenced resource that caters to a diverse audience with its clear and simple language. Each chapter delivers actionable insights, transforming theory into practical applications and making this book an invaluable guide for enhancing business communication skills."

— **Zunder Lal**,
Co-Founder and CTO - OpenTurf Technologies

"An empowering blueprint for mastering business communication, this book unlocks the mindset, skillset, and strategies to command influence and impact. A game-changer for professionals, it transforms corporate conversations into powerful leadership tools."

— **Dr. Prabodh**,
Chairman of All India Food
Processing Association, Western region

"Communication is the very foundation of any relationship though low context and high context cultures communicate differently. Relationships play an important role in business decisions & communication decides the fate of any relationship. Kudos to Preeti for handling such a topic with the blend of strategy, sensitivity and empathy."

— **Dr Amit Nagpal**,
Story Coach, Speaker and Bestselling Author

"When I look back, I remember struggling with shyness and seeing English as a huge barrier. Over time, I realized that communication isn't just about language - it's about confidence and clarity. The simple yet powerful strategies in Preeti's book can help overcome hesitation and unlock the endless opportunities that come with effective communication."

— **Shaifaly Sangal**,
Founder & CEO - Yung Minds,
Author & Ho'oponopono Healer

"What I love about this book is its perfect blend of mindset coaching and practical strategies that help non-native speakers build confidence while mastering English. The easy-to-understand approach and relatable examples make it an invaluable tool for anyone wanting to overcome their language learning challenges."

— **Gauri Das**,
SVP and Head HR, TEDx Speaker
LinkedIn Top Voice

"Like a comprehensive course in your hands, it covers everything a modern business professional needs - from handling daily workplace talks to mastering high-stakes negotiations and global team dynamics."

— **Rupali Srivastav**,
Head Learning, Talent & CSR at Care Edge

STRATEGIC BUSINESS COMMUNICATION

STRATEGIC BUSINESS COMMUNICATION

Speak Like A Global Leader

Elevate your English, Maximize your Impact

Preeti Subberwal

KB
INTERNATIONAL

First published by **Naveen Chand Kabdwal for Kabdwal Book International (KBI Publishers) in 2025.**

INTERNATIONAL

Kabdwal Book International
TEX Centre Premises, Unit No. L – 3, 4, 5 & 6
4th Floor, Narayan Plaza
26-A, Chandivali Road, Near Boomerang Building,
Andheri East, Mumbai 400 072, Maharashtra, India
www.kabdwalbook.com / www.kbipublishers.com

Name: Subberwal Preeti
Title: Strategic Business Communication: Speak Like a Global Leader - Elevate your English, Maximize your Impact / Preeti Subberwal.
Printed by SAP Print Solutions Pvt. Ltd, Mumbai 400013 India

ISBN: 978-81-984-6584-9 (PB)

KBI Team: Rajesh Raheja, Syed Husain Mendhdi Naqvi

In cherished memory of my beloved mother - Mrs. Anupam Nagpal,
my first English teacher and my lifelong guiding light.
Her love for English became the foundation of my journey, shaping my path in ways I could never have imagined.

Foreword

I studied in a Hindi-medium school. And here I am today, writing the foreword for a book on **Strategic Business Communication** that too in English.

It took me years to break the mental barrier that held me back from speaking English with confidence. For the longest time, I felt I was not "good enough" at it. But as I grew in my career, I realized something surprising. I was not alone.

Just last weekend, I met a friend who is the CEO of a well-known brand. Over coffee, he confessed something that caught me off guard. He had also struggled with English communication. Despite being a successful leader, he carried the same insecurity I once did.

It was hard for me to believe that he struggled with English communication as well. He told me that every time he spoke a sentence, he worried whether his English was correct. And that made him lose confidence. He even took English-speaking classes to fix this problem. When he became a father, he made sure his daughter Ria studied in the best English medium school, so she would never feel the way he did.

One day, Ria accompanied him to an office event. The chief guest was an Italian business leader who delivered an inspiring speech. My friend was impressed. But after the event, Ria made an observation that changed his perspective forever. She said, *"Dad, none of the speakers today spoke perfect English. But they all spoke with confidence. And that is why they sounded so good."*

That was the moment my friend realized, communication is not about speaking perfect English. It is about speaking with confidence, clarity, and impact. From that day on, he stopped worrying about small mistakes and started owning his words.

His story is not unique. I have seen some of the brightest professionals, industry leaders, experts, and visionaries struggle to express their ideas with the same confidence they have in their knowledge. And in today's global business world, that is a real problem. Because communication is not just about knowing a language. It is about using it strategically to influence, connect, and lead.

This is why **Strategic Business Communication** is such an important book. It does not just teach you English. It shows you how to **own the conversation**, whether you are leading a team, pitching an idea, or managing a high-stakes negotiation.

Preeti Subberwal has distilled years of experience into simple, powerful strategies that anyone can apply. There is no overload of theory, just practical tools that will help you **speak with confidence, clarity, and conviction** in real business situations.

What I love most about this book is its **real-world approach**. It is not just about learning English. It is about **mastering the art of business communication**. By the time you finish reading, you won't just *feel* more confident. You'll be **ready to step up, speak up, and stand out**.

Because at the end of the day, leadership is not just about **what you know**. It is about **how well you communicate what you know**. This book will help you do just that.

Harjeet Khanduja
HR Mastermind

Preface

Dear Reader,

Ever noticed how some of the brightest minds in the room stay silent in meetings?

We see it every day - brilliant professionals struggling to find the right words in English. Tech wizards who can code in five languages but hesitate to speak in one. Strategic masterminds who design complex solutions but struggle to influence global stakeholders. Seasoned leaders who dominate domestic markets but lose their impact in global forums.

Across the corporate landscape, groundbreaking ideas go unspoken, innovation gets lost in translation, and leadership potential remains untapped–not due to a lack of talent, but because of nagging voice that whispers, "My English isn't good enough."

Years of coaching professionals and entrepreneurs have taught me one thing: the key to powerful global communication isn't just fluency in English - it's mastering strategic communication.

This book isn't about sounding like a native speaker; it's about communicating like a confident global leader. Inside, you'll find practical, results-driven techniques that have helped thousands of professionals elevate their leadership presence. No theoretical fluff - just actionable strategies that work in high- stakes business environments

Whether you're leading multinational teams, shaping global strategy, or building international alliances, this book is your blueprint for mastering strategic communication.

Let's transform your communication into your leadership signature!

Warm Regards
Preeti

A New Paradigm for Mastering Business English

Remember those English classes in school? Grammar rules, vocabulary lists, and endless essays. Now you're in the corporate world, and it's a whole new ballgame. Knowing English isn't enough anymore. The real challenge? Using it to wow in meetings, nail presentations, and craft killer emails.

That's where the **mindset, skillset, and toolset** approach comes in. Developing the right **mindset** builds confidence and overcome barriers, the right **skillset** refines your language proficiency and delivery, and the right **toolset** equips you with practical techniques to apply in real-world scenarios. Together, they ensure you start commanding influence in any business setting.

They say, "*Practice makes you perfect.*" I believe, "*Perfect practice makes you perfect.*" It's not about the hours you put in, but the strategy behind every interaction, presentation, and keynote speaking. Success comes from practicing with purpose and precision, let me show you where we're heading:

First Stop: The Inner Game (Chapter 1 | MINDSET MAGIC) We start where success really begins - in your mind. Before diving into techniques, we'll break down those mental barriers holding you back and make the required shift in the mindset.

Building Your Foundation (Chapter 2–3 | GRAMMAR MADE EASY & VERBAL TOOLBOX) Next, we'll tackle the essentials you'll actually use in business settings - no theoretical overload, just what works in real situations.

Finding Your Flow (Chapter 4–5 | STRUCTURING CONVERSATIONS & POWER OF EXPRESSION) This is where it gets exciting - you'll learn to express yourself naturally and confidently. We move from correct English to impactful English, from forming sentences to telling compelling business stories.

Navigating Complex Waters (Chapter 6–7 | CULTURAL CONNECTORS & POISE UNDER PRESSURE) Now we enter advanced territory - handling cultural nuances and difficult conversations. This is where good communicators become great leaders, turning potential conflicts into opportunities for connection.

The Leadership Summit (Chapter 8–9 | FORGE CONNECTIONS & EXECUTIVE COMMUNICATION) This is where all elements converge into your leadership presence. You will learn to influence global stakeholders, build cross-cultural relationships, and lead with authentic authority.

Tailor your Communication (Chapter 10 | STRATEGIES AND SCRIPTS FOR BUSINESS FUNCTIONS) Finally, you'll discover tailored communication strategies and ready-to-use scripts designed to meet the specific needs of various departments.

Whether you're facing your boss one-on-one or presenting to a room full of execs, each chapter builds on the previous one, just like your growing confidence will build on each small success.

You'll find real examples from corporate professionals who've walked this path, practical exercises you can use immediately, and strategies that work in actual business situations.

Ready to transform your communication game? It's time to speak the language of success.

Contents

Introduction:
The Power of Business English

Mastering Business English is your ticket to career advancement, whether you're a fresh grad or a seasoned pro. In today's interconnected world, Business English is the universal language of success. From Silicon Valley startups to centuries-old corporations, from bustling trading floors to virtual boardrooms, English serves as the bridge that connects ambitious professionals across continents. It's the language that turns local talent into global leaders.

The Professional Edge: Where Business English Makes the Difference

As you strive for professional growth, strong Business English skills play a vital role at some of these critical moments.

1. **Leading Meetings**: Transforming from a passive participant into a confident voice that shapes decisions and drives outcomes.
2. **Powerful Presentations**: Commanding attention, not just through slides, but through stories that resonate and persuade across cultural boundaries.
3. **Effective Emails:** Writing clear, concise, and impactful emails that convey professionalism, drive action, and leave a lasting impression.
4. **Strategic Communication**: Craft messages that cut through the noise, whether in crucial meetings, comprehensive reports, or quick chats.

5. **Global Networking**: Build authentic connections that transcend borders, creating a professional network that opens doors worldwide.
6. **Client Excellence**: Turn client interactions into lasting partnerships through clear, confident, and culturally aware communication.
7. **Leadership Impact**: Guide teams with clarity and inspiration, regardless of their cultural or linguistic backgrounds.

The Building Blocks of Business English Excellence

Mastering Business English involves developing a range of skills and competencies:

1. **Verbal and Vocal Communication**: Speaking clearly, confidently, and persuasively in various professional settings. Learn to modulate your tone, pace, and emphasis to ensure your message not only reaches but resonates with your audience.
2. **Written Communication**: From crafting compelling proposals to writing persuasive reports, develop the skills to make your written communication work for you, not against you.
3. **Business Vocabulary**: Build a rich repository of industry-specific terminology and professional expressions that position you as a credible voice in your field.
4. **Listening Skills**: Develop the crucial skill of understanding not just words, but intentions. Learn to navigate different accents, grasp cultural nuances, and read between the lines in professional contexts.
5. **Presentation and Negotiation Skills**: Master the art of turning information into inspiration with powerful presentation skills and persuasive negotiation language. Learn techniques to create memorable experiences, resolve conflicts, and achieve win-win outcomes in any professional setting.

6. **Cross-Cultural Communication**: Develop the awareness and skills to navigate cultural differences effectively, turning potential barriers into bridges for successful international collaboration.
7. **Non-Verbal Communication**: Master the unspoken elements of professional communication - from body language to facial expressions that can either reinforce or undermine your message.

CHAPTER 1

Mindset Magic: Building English Speaking Success

We all have that little voice in our heads that says we're not good enough or that learning English is too hard. But think about successful people you know who have learned English as a second language. They didn't let those thoughts hold them back. You can do the same.

In this chapter, we will install some empowering beliefs that will help you navigate your English language journey with confidence, enthusiasm, and resilience. The key is to stay positive, stay motivated, and keep moving forward toward your goals.

Tackling Your English Brain Blocks

Meet Raj and Sofia, co-workers at a global tech company.

Raj fears speaking English. In meetings, he's silent. Giving updates makes him sweat. He thinks, "*I'll never sound as good as the others.*"

Sofia sees English as a fun challenge. She speaks up in meetings, even if she makes mistakes. Preparing presentations is her chance to try new words. She believes, "*Every error helps me improve.*"

Fast forward a year. Raj is still hiding behind his monitor, while Sofia's giving a TED talk on AI ethics.

The lesson? Your attitude shapes your progress

Let's break them down and build you up:

1. **The Perfectionist Trap**: First off, forget perfection. It's a myth, like unicorns or calorie-free cake. Native speakers make mistakes all the time. Aim for progress, not perfection. It's not about being "good at English" or "bad at English." It's about being "getting better at business English." Every conversation is practice. Every mistake is a lesson.
2. **The Doubt Monster**: "I'll mess up!" It loves to pop up right before big meetings. But remember, even native speakers stumble sometimes. Your ideas matter more than perfect grammar.
3. **The Comparison Game**: Fluent colleagues got you feeling down! Remember, they started somewhere too. Your journey is unique, and every small improvement is a victory.
4. **The Comfort Zone Cling**: Sticking to your native language feels safe, but growth happens outside that bubble. Each English interaction, no matter how small, builds your confidence.
5. **The Ghost of English Past**: Bad experiences can haunt us, but they don't define your future. Those moments were lessons, not failures.

From Doubt to Confidence: Your Mindset Makeover

Dedicate just fifteen minutes daily to deliberate practice. Have conversations in the mirror while getting ready. Track your journey with purpose by keeping a simple "wins journal." Document breakthrough moments and positive feedback.

When doubt creeps in, add "yet" to your thoughts. "I can't nail that presentation" becomes "I can't nail that presentation... yet!"

It's time to reframe your beliefs and accelerate your language learning progress with the help of suggestions in Table 1.1.

Table 1.1

When You Think...	Try This Instead...	Power Move
English is too complicated to master.	I can learn what I need to step by step.	Break learning into small, manageable goals. Take baby steps.
I need perfect grammar to speak.	I need clear ideas to contribute.	Focus on your message, not just the mechanics.
Native speakers will judge my mistakes.	Professional value comes from ideas, not perfect grammar.	Focus on clear communication using your expertise.
They won't understand my English.	I'll find ways to make my points clear.	Use examples and analogies to strengthen understanding.
I find it difficult to choose the right words to express myself.	I'm expanding my vocabulary naturally.	Every new word is a tool, not a test.
I can't learn because I'm too old.	My experience gives me more context for learning.	Use your professional knowledge as a foundation for language learning.
I freeze during important presentations.	I prepare well and improve with practice.	Each presentation makes you stronger.
It takes years to speak well.	Every conversation makes me better.	Set 90-day improvement targets instead of thinking years ahead.
I don't have enough time.	I can learn during my daily work.	Integrate learning into your current schedule - no extra time needed.
My English isn't good enough for leadership.	My ideas and experience qualify me to lead.	Leadership is about impact, not perfect English.

Practice Drill: List any doubts or limiting beliefs you have about your English skills. Then think of those who have successfully navigated similar challenges.

Keep reminding yourself that every English pro was once a beginner. Your journey to fluency is a marathon, not a sprint. Take it one conversation at a time!

The Four Stage of Your Learning Journey

Ever wonder why learning English feels like a rollercoaster? Let's break it down:

1. **Unconscious Incompetence:** You don't know what you don't know.
   In a business meeting, you say "Please revert back to me" (which is redundant) or "I will discuss about the project" (incorrect preposition), unaware these are non-native expressions.
2. **Conscious Incompetence:** You know what you don't know! You've learned that "revert" means "return to a previous state" and not "reply," and that "discuss" doesn't need "about." You catch yourself making these mistakes in emails but still struggle to remember the correct forms under pressure.
3. **Conscious Competence:** You know what you know.
   You carefully write "Please get back to me" in emails and say "Let's discuss the project" in meetings, mentally checking your business vocabulary and common phrases before speaking.
4. **Unconscious Competence:** You don't know what you know. You confidently lead conference calls, seamlessly using phrases like "Let me follow up on that," "I'll get back to you by EOD," and "Could we circle back to the first point?" without second-guessing your word choice.

Everyone starts at stage 1. Whether you're fumbling in the dark or smoothly cruising, you're right where you need to be. Keep pushing, your next level is just around the corner!

Know Your Why: Your English North Star

Ever wonder why some people seem to breeze through English learning while others struggle? The secret often lies in their "why."

As Tony Robbins puts it, "If there is a big enough why, you figure out how."

Your "why" is your personal rocket fuel. It's what gets you out of bed for that 6 AM English podcast, or keeps you practicing presentations in front of the mirror. Maybe you dream of wowing clients in international meetings, or perhaps you've got your eye on that promotion that requires fluent English. Whatever it is, make it vivid in your mind.

Take Rajesh, for example. This software whiz wasn't just learning English for fun. He had a clear vision of becoming a global project manager. That dream pushed him through tough conference calls and late night study sessions. He zeroed in on the exact English skills he needed - tech lingo and presentation prowess. The result? Within a year, he was confidently leading calls with US and UK clients and earned a promotion.

Your turn: What's your English "why"? Jot it down, make it specific, and let it be your guiding star. Whether it's nailing that dream job interview or confidently presenting at a global conference, your "why" will keep you going when the going gets tough.

Setting SMART Goals for English Proficiency

Vague goals like "become fluent" can be overwhelming. SMART goals provide clarity and motivation.

1. **Specificity**: Focus on precise areas. e.g.: "Improve business email writing skills."
2. **Measurability**: Define clear criteria. e.g.: "Have 10-minute conversations in English daily."
3. **Achievability**: Set ambitious yet realistic goals. e.g.: "Learn 20 new industry-specific terms weekly."
4. **Relevance**: Align with overall objectives. e.g.: "Practice presentation skills for upcoming conference."

5. **Time-bound**: Set specific deadlines. e.g.: "Achieve B2 level proficiency in 6 months."

Examples of SMART English Goals

1. Speaking Fluently: "I will have a 10-minute conversation in English without long pauses, three times a week for the next month."
2. Increasing Vocabulary: "I will learn and use 10 new business-related English words each week for the next three months."
3. Improving Presentation Skills: "I will deliver a 5-minute presentation in English to my team by the end of this quarter."

Your Turn: Set one SMART goal for your English learning journey. Write it down and place it somewhere you'll see daily.

Building Confidence in Communication

Think of confidence in Business English like learning to drive. At first, every move feels calculated and nerve-wracking, but eventually, it becomes your second nature. Your journey to confident English communication doesn't have to be overwhelming. Let's break it down into actionable strategies that work.

The Confidence Blueprint

1. **Start Small, Dream Big**
   Begin with bite-sized challenges. Something as simple as sending a quick email to a colleague can build momentum. Each small win strengthens your confidence muscle, preparing you for bigger challenges ahead.
2. **Embrace an English Lifestyle**
   Wake up to English news with your coffee. Jam to English podcasts on your commute. Swap your phone's language to English. Wind down with an English book or show. These

small habits add up, turning English from a chore into a natural part of your day.

3. **Build Your Support System**
   Confidence thrives in the right environment. Find a language accountability partner who shares your professional goals. Connect with mentors who've walked your path. Create safe spaces where you can practice without judgment.
4. **Leverage Technology Wisely**
   Turn your devices into confidence-building tools. Record yourself speaking to analyse and improve your presentation skills. Use writing assistants to draft emails more confidently. Regular video calls with international colleagues can provide practical experience in a controlled environment.
5. **Self-Reflection and Assessment**
   Regularly pause to assess your progress. It's like checking your GPS on a road trip – it helps you see how far you've come and plan your next moves. Celebrate every new word, every successful conversation. They're all victories on your path to fluency.

The Golden Rule: Confidence isn't about never making mistakes, it's about knowing that you can handle them when they happen. Your journey to confident communication starts with one conversation at a time.

The Aisha Effect:
Meet Aisha, your resilience role model. Her first big presentation? A total flop. But instead of giving up, she:

- Dissected her performance to identify improvement areas
- Sought honest feedback from colleagues
- Enlisted help from a presentation pro
- Built confidence through smaller speaking engagements

The result? Six months later, Aisha delivered a knockout presentation that landed a major client.

Chapter Wrap-Up: Mindset Matters!

Quick Action Plan:

1. **Daily Boost**: Read your "I can" statements each morning.
2. **Set Mini-Goals**: Pick three situations to boost your English. Set small, doable targets.
3. **Weekly Win List:** Jot down three English improvements, no matter how tiny.
4. **Monthly Challenge:** Do one thing that scares you in English.
5. **Reflect and Reset**: Review progress, celebrate wins, learn from setbacks, set new SMART goals.

Resilience isn't about never falling; it's about rising every time you fall. Your English journey will have ups and downs, but with persistence, you'll reach heights you never imagined.

As we close this chapter, carry this thought with you: Your determination is your greatest asset. Every word you learn, every conversation you have, is a step forward. Keep pushing, keep learning, and watch as your English skills and confidence soar. Your future fluent self is rooting for you!

CHAPTER 2

Grammar Made Easy: Navigating the Essentials of Grammar

In a world of rapid-fire Slack messages and quick emails, grammar can feel like that friend who's a bit too proper for the party. Here's the thing about grammar - it's not about impressing your old English teacher or winning a spelling bee. It's about getting your message across clearly.

Think of grammar like the rules of the road. You don't need to know every traffic law by heart to be a good driver. You just need to know enough to get where you're going safely and efficiently.

In this chapter, we'll focus on what actually matters in day-to-day business communication. No fancy linguistic terms, no obscure rules - just practical guidance that you can use in your next meeting or presentation.

The Building Blocks of Language

Nouns and Pronouns: The Who and What of It

Think of nouns as the main characters in your business story - your teams, clients and products and pronouns are their stand-ins.

- **Human Resources** collaborated with **IT**, and streamlined the **employee** onboarding process.
- **TechSols** reviewed their **service package**, and customized it to meet the **client's** specific needs.
- The **marketing team** developed their quarterly **strategy**, and presented it confidently to the leadership.

Verbs: Unlock the Action Words

These are your power moves in business speak.

- Marketing transformed our digital engagement strategy.
- She **navigated** complex negotiation challenges.
- They **pioneered** a breakthrough approach.
- We **implemented** cutting-edge machine learning algorithms.

Pro Tips:

- Choose Active Over Passive: Drove project success through direct, ownership-driven language.
- Be Specific: Instead of saying, "Do the work" use words like Execute, Implement, Streamline
- Show Impact: "Worked on sales" can be substituted by "accelerated revenue generation by 25%."
- Use strong action verbs like transformed, optimized, pioneered, revolutionized and elevated.
- Avoid weak fillers like helped and assisted, and replace them with led, drove and spearheaded.
- Quantify when possible like reduced costs by 40% and increased efficiency by 2x.
- Match Verbs to Context:
    - **Meetings**: Facilitated, Coordinated, Moderated, Structured, Navigated, Aligned
    - **Projects**: Developed, Implemented, Executed, Managed, Launched, Designed
    - **Sales**: Generated, Converted, Expanded, Accelerated, Secured, Negotiated
    - **Leadership**: Guided, Inspired, Championed, Elevated, Empowered, Steered

Adjectives and Adverbs: The Spice Rack

- **Powerful Descriptors**: strategic, innovative, comprehensive, collaborative, efficient, groundbreaking, market-disrupting solution, streamlined, cost-optimizing process

- Avoiding Weak Intensifiers like really important; use words like critical, crucial, and pivotal
- **Action-Oriented Descriptors**: Use phrases like proactively developed, systematically implemented and strategically aligned.
- **Domain-Specific Modifiers:**
    - **Tech**: Scalable, Agile, Robust, Innovative, Cutting-edge, Future-ready
    - **Finance**: Strategic, Analytical, Predictive, Data-driven, Results-oriented
    - **Marketing**: Targeted, Engaging, Conversion-focused, Customer-centric, Brand-building

Prepositions: Connecting Ideas in Space and Time

These little words (in, on, at, by, with) are tricky.

Real Mix-ups you often hear:

- Let's collaborate with completing this (Nope, "collaborate on")
- Different to what we planned (Nope, "different from")
- We're going in LinkedIn (Nope, "going on")
- We'll discuss about the project (Nope, just "discuss the project")
- Aligned to common goals (use towards instead of to)

Conjunctions: Your Sentence Superglue

And, but, or, yet, moreover etc. - they're the traffic lights of your sentences. Use them to guide your listener smoothly.

- The project faced significant challenges, **yet** we delivered exceptional results.
- Budget constraints were tight, **but** our team's creativity prevailed.
- Initial strategies failed, **however**, we quickly adapted.

- The team worked remotely, **moreover**, productivity increased by 30%.
- We launched the new product line, **additionally**, we opened three new markets.

Articles (a, an, the): The Subtle Art of Specificity

Mastering articles can be tricky, but it's crucial for sounding natural in English.

- She is **the** employee of the month.
- He is **an** expert in digital marketing.
- The company received **a** prestigious award for innovation.
- We need **the** approval of senior management before proceeding.
- Please send me **the** latest sales report.

Use "the" for specific items, "a/an" for general ones, and no article for broad concepts or plural generalities.

And don't beat yourself up when you notice some grammar slips - we all have them. Just notice patterns and pick ONE thing to work on at a time.

Mastering Tenses in Professional Communication

Tenses convey when actions occur, ensuring clarity and accuracy in business communication. Refer to the Table 2.1 for their usage.

Key Points:

- Choose tenses based on the action's timeframe and relationship to other events.
- Maintain tense consistency within contexts for clarity.
- Use time markers: "currently", "previously", "in the future"
- Use present tense for timeless facts or company policies.

- Past tense is common in reports or discussing completed projects.
- Future tense helps in strategic planning and goal-setting discussions.

Table 2.1

1. Present Tense		
Tense	**Usage**	**Example**
Simple	Habits, general truths	Our company prioritizes customer satisfaction.
Continuous	Ongoing actions	We are currently reviewing the proposal.
Perfect	Completed actions with present relevance	The team has finished the quarterly report.
2. Past Tense		
Simple	Completed past actions	The meeting concluded at 3 PM yesterday.
Continuous	Ongoing past actions	We were developing the strategy when the market shifted.
Perfect	Actions completed before another past event	By the time the CEO arrived, we had prepared the presentation.
3. Future Tense		
Simple	Planned future actions	The company will launch the new product next month.
Continuous	Ongoing future actions	This time next week, we'll be presenting at the conference.

Crafting Clear and Impactful Sentences

Craft clear and concise sentences using varied structures to maintain the interest of your audience.

- Despite the challenges, she remained resilient.
- The project was completed ahead of schedule, exceeding expectations.
- To succeed in this competitive industry, you must adapt quickly.

- He not only leads the team but also mentors junior staff.
- By analysing market trends, we can anticipate customer needs.

Negation

Understand how to express negation using words like 'not,' 'never,' and 'no' to convey denial or contradiction accurately. Misplaced negation can lead to misunderstandings.

- I **don't** have any prior experience in this field.
- There **isn't** any room for error in this project.
- He **never** misses an opportunity to learn and grow.
- They **won't** be attending the conference next month.
- We **can't** afford to overlook this issue any longer.

Subject-Verb Agreement: Ensuring Clarity

Singular subjects take singular verbs; plural subjects take plural verbs. Ensure that the subject and verb in your sentences agree in number and person.

- **The team** is collaborating on the new project.
- **Our marketing department** meets every Monday for brainstorming sessions.
- **She** knows the importance of punctuality.
- **The company** has experienced rapid growth in recent years.
- **He** works diligently to meet deadlines.

Sentence Structure: From Simple to Complex

Understanding the three sentence types (simple, compound, complex) allows you to vary your expression and maintain audience engagement.

1. **Simple Sentences Definition**: Simple sentences are direct and impactful.
    - One independent clause (subject + verb)

Examples:

- "The report is ready."
- "Our team exceeded targets."
- "The CEO approved the budget."

2. **Complex Sentences** add depth and nuance to communication. One independent clause + one or more dependent clauses Examples:
   - o "Although the market is volatile, our investments remain stable."
   - o "When the new system is implemented, productivity should increase."
   - o "If sales continue to grow, we'll expand our operations."
3. **Compound Sentences** balance related ideas.
   Two or more independent clauses joined by coordinating conjunctions
   Examples:
   - o "The project is on schedule, but costs are higher than anticipated."
   - o "We can accept the offer, or we can negotiate further."
   - o "The client loved our presentation, so we're likely to win the contract."

   Effective Usage:
   - Vary sentence structures to maintain reader engagement.
   - Use simple sentences for emphasis or clear directives.
   - Employ complex sentences to explain relationships or provide context.
   - Utilize compound sentences to connect closely related ideas.

Types of Sentences: Declarative, Interrogative, Imperative, and Exclamatory

Think of these sentence types as tools in your communication toolkit. Here's the breakdown in Table 2.2, with real examples I've collected from actual workplace situations.

Table 2.2

Type	What It Does	Email Example	Presentation Example	When to Use & Pro Tips
Declarative	States facts or opinions	The deadline is Friday.	Our market share grew 15%.	• Use for clear information sharing • Great for setting context • Your go-to for most business communication
Interrogative	Asks questions	Could you review this?	What challenges are you facing?	• Perfect for engagement • Softens requests • Shows interest
Imperative	Gives commands or requests	Please respond ASAP.	Sign up for our newsletter.	• Use sparingly in emails • Add "please" to soften • Great for Call to Action
Exclamatory	Shows strong emotion	Thanks for your help!	We've hit our target!	• Use rarely in business • Keep professional • Perfect for celebrations

Reported Speech: Conveying Information Professionally

1. Direct Speech preserves original wording and tone and reports exact words within quotation marks
   Examples:
   - The CEO announced, "We will be expanding into the Asian market next quarter."
   - "Our team needs to improve communication," the manager stated in the meeting.
   - The client said, "We're very satisfied with the results of the campaign."
2. Indirect Speech conveys the essence of what was said and paraphrases or summarizes without quotation marks Examples:
   - The CEO announced that they would be expanding into the Asian market the following quarter.

  - The manager stated in the meeting that their team needed to improve communication.
  - The client said that they were very satisfied with the results of the campaign.

Refer to Table 2.3 for the usage guidelines for reported speech

Table 2.3

Context	Preferred Speech	Reason
Formal reports	Indirect	Conciseness and objectivity
Meeting minutes	Indirect	Summarizing key points
Legal documentation	Direct	Accuracy and precision
Motivational messages	Direct	Preserving impact and tone
Performance reviews	Mix of both	Balance between details and summary
Email communication	Depends on formality	Direct for emphasis, indirect for brevity

Direct speech captures exact words and tone while indirect speech summarizes the message. Choose based on context, audience, and purpose of your communication.

Punctuation: The Rhythm and Clarity of English

Punctuation guides your reader through your ideas. Master the use of commas, periods, semicolons, and colons to organize your ideas and clarify your message. Proper punctuation enhances readability and professionalism.

- The presentation was informative, engaging, and well-prepared.
- Please send me the report by Friday. I need it for the meeting.
- After the merger, productivity declined, profits decreased, and morale suffered.
- In conclusion, I believe we can achieve our goals if we work together.
- The CEO's message was clear, concise, and inspiring.

Modals: Expressing Possibility, Obligation, and Permission

Modals are auxiliary verbs that modify the main verb to express possibility, probability, permission, or obligation. They add depth and politeness to professional communication.

1. Can/Could (Ability, Possibility, Permission)
   - "Can you submit the report by Friday?" (Polite request)
   - "We could potentially increase sales by 15%." (Possibility)
2. May/Might (Possibility, Permission)
   - "May I schedule a meeting with you?" (Polite permission)
   - "The project might be delayed due to unforeseen circumstances." (Possibility)
3. Must/Should (Obligation, Strong Recommendation)
   - "All employees must attend the safety training." (Obligation)
   - "We should consider diversifying our product line." (Recommendation)
4. Will/Would (Future Actions, Polite Requests)
   - "The CEO will announce the merger next week." (Future certainty)
   - "Would you be interested in leading the new project?" (Polite inquiry)
5. Shall/Ought to (Suggestions, Moral Obligation)
   - "Shall we break for lunch?" (Suggestion)
   - "The company ought to prioritize sustainability." (Moral obligation)

Note: Modals don't change form for different subjects. They help express varying degrees of certainty or formality.

Examples:

1) We can finish the project. (ability)
2) We could finish the project. (possibility)
3) We should finish the project. (advice/obligation)

4) We must finish the project. (strong obligation)
5) We might finish the project. (uncertainty)

Conditionals: Discussing Hypotheticals and Consequences

Conditionals are crucial for discussing hypothetical situations, making proposals, and negotiating.

Three Main Conditionals

1. First Conditional (Likely future): If we increase production, we will meet the deadline.
2. Second Conditional (Unlikely/imaginary present): If I were the CEO, I would implement a four-day workweek.
3. Third Conditional (Impossible past): If we had invested in that startup, we would have made a significant profit.

Common Grammar Pitfalls to Avoid

I've messed up most of these at some point. We all do. Here's how to catch them before they catch you!

Table 2.4 illustrates some common offenders:

Table 2.4

Category	Wrong	Right
Their/They're/ There	Their going to the meeting.	They're going to the meeting.
Who's/Whose	Who's presentation is this?	Whose presentation is this?
Its/It's	The company and it's employees.	The company and its employees.
Affect/Effect	This will effect our sales.	This will affect our sales. (Affect=Verb, Effect=Noun)
Less/Fewer	Less people attended	Fewer people attended
Who/Whom	Who did you give it to	To whom did you give it?
Me/I	Between you and I	Between you and me

Chapter Wrap Up: Grammar as Your Communication Foundation

Whatever has been covered in the chapter aren't rigid rules; they're more like guidelines for not sounding like a robot. Trust your ear, and when in doubt, read it out loud. If you stumble, your audience probably will too.

Before hitting 'send' or speaking up, take that quick gut check:

- Is it clear? (If you stumble reading it, your audience will too)
- Is it active? (Make those verbs work for their money)
- Would you actually say it this way? (If not, rewrite it)

Think of grammar like your business outfit - it should be professional enough to be taken seriously, but not so stiff that you can't move. You want people focusing on your ideas, not counting your grammar slip-ups.

1. **Master the Building Blocks:** Understanding your language tools isn't about rules – it's about power. Each element helps you build precise, impactful messages.
2. **Structure for Impact:** Clear sentences aren't born; they're built. Subject-verb agreement, proper structure, and strategic voice choice create messages that land with clarity and purpose.
3. **Add Sophistication Through Tools:** Use advanced tools like modals, conditionals, and relative clauses to express possibilities, explore scenarios, and deepen descriptions.
4. **Command Your Tenses:** Master tenses to show not just when things happen, but their relationship to each other and their impact.
5. **Choose Your Voice:** Choose active to drive action, passive to focus on results or maintain diplomacy.

When your grammar foundations are strong, your ideas flow freely, and your message lands exactly as intended.

Chapter 3

Craft Your Verbal Toolbox: Converse Like a Pro

"I just can't find the right words!" If I had a dollar for every time a client told me this, I'd be writing this from my private island. We've all been there - that perfect idea stuck in your head, but your mouth's gone blank.

Words do matter in business; they can make or break deals, inspire teams, or spark innovation. In this chapter, we'll crack the code on choosing words that land appropriately, s, and speaking with the kind of confidence that makes people lean in and listen. No fancy linguistics degree is required - just real-world tools that work when it matters most.

The Foundation: Active Listening

Ever felt like you're talking to a brick wall in a meeting? That's the opposite of active listening, and it's costing businesses big time.

Active listening isn't just hearing; it's understanding the whole message - words, tone, and even what's not being said.

Here's your roadmap to becoming an active listening pro:

1. **Full attention:** Eyes on the speaker, phone away. Simple, but game-changing.
2. **Show engagement:** Nod, maintain eye contact, use brief verbal cues like "I see."

3. **No interruptions:** Let them finish. Your turn will come.
4. **Reflect and clarify:** "So, you're saying..." This ensures you're on the same wavelength.
5. **Ask thoughtful questions:** "Could you elaborate on that?" Shows genuine interest.

In meetings, when a colleague shares a concern, focus fully. Respond with, *"It sounds like the deadline is causing stress. How can we tackle this together?"* With clients, after they outline needs, confirm: "*So, you need X done by Y date with Z features. Have I got that right?*"

Take it a step further with empathetic listening. Try to understand their feelings and perspectives. It's like putting on their shoes and walking a mile in those shoes so that you know where the shoe pinches.

Let's face it - even the best of us falls into listening traps. There's that constant phone buzz during crucial conversations, the temptation to jump to conclusions before someone's finished, the mental rehearsal of our brilliant response while missing half the actual message, and that moment when our brain hits overload and just can't process one more piece of information.

But here's the deal: great listeners aren't born - they're built. Put the phone away, catch yourself when you're prejudging, actually listen instead of planning your response, and when it's information overload, don't hesitate to ask for a quick recap. Because in business, the person who truly listens often becomes the person others trust to lead.

Building Your Vocabulary Arsenal

Ever freeze up searching for the right word in a big meeting? You're not alone. However, building your word power doesn't have to feel like cramming for a difficult exam.

Here's how to beef up your business vocabulary without the textbook torture

- Make your commute work for you. Plug into business podcasts where industry leaders share real stories. Pure gold for picking up current business speak.
- Got your phone handy? Use language apps like Duolingo. Think of them as your pocket vocab coach.
- Create a "power words" list in your Notes app. Heard your CEO use a term that made everyone sit up straight? Jot it down. That client who always nails their presentations? Steal their phrases.
- Start a "word of the week" challenge with your team. Someone drops a cool business term, everyone tries to use it naturally.
- Read like your next promotion depends on it - because it might. Industry blogs, reports, even those company-wide emails from leadership. They're all vocab goldmines.
- Watch everything with English subtitles on - yes, everything. Your brain catches words dif-ferently when you read and hear them together.
- Hit up LinkedIn for 10 minutes daily. Follow industry big shots - their posts are packed with current business language. Plus, you'll stay on top of what's trending.
- Subscribe to a few solid business newsletters. Scan them during your morning coffee. The good ones pack punchy language that's worth borrowing.

Pro Tip: Create a personal "word bank" in a notebook or digital app. Categorize words by business situations (e.g., negotiation, presentation, small talk) for easy reference.

Whether you're pitching to clients or rallying your team, having the right words at your fingertips can turn a good message into one that sticks. Remember, Rome wasn't built in a day, and neither is a killer vocabulary. Keep at it, and soon you'll be slinging business lingo like a pro!

Choosing the Right Words: Precision in Communication

I once saw a CFO turn a rambling 20-page report into a crisp 5- pager. It was like magic. She cut the corporate speak and got to the point. The board loved it.

Rahul from marketing turned "We need to improve our online presence" into "*We'll increase our website traffic by 30% this quarter through targeted SEO and content marketing.*"

I once had a client, Priyanka, who struggled with this. In emails, she'd write, "The project had issues." Vague, right? We worked on precision. Now she writes, "*The project faced a two-week delay due to supply chain disruptions.*"

Here are some tricks that I've picked up over the years:

- Ditch the corporate buzzwords. Nobody needs to hear about "leveraging synergies." Just say "working together."
- Get specific with deadlines. "Soon" means nothing. "By next Tuesday" means everything.
- Be real about problems. Instead of "facing challenges," say "We're over budget by 15%."
- Balance accessibility and expertise as per your audience. In presentations, use language that engages both the tech guru and the intern. eg. "*We're adding bank-level security to protect your data, making it virtually impossible to crack.*"
- Empathize in sensitive talks: When addressing issues with colleagues, choose words that show you care, not just criticize. eg. "*Would you be open to exploring some techniques that could make your presentations even more impactful?*"

Here are strong examples captured in Table 3.1 that show clear impact

Table 3.1

Vague	Specific & Impactful
Had a productive discussion	Secured $500K budget approval for Q2 project
Making good progress	Completed 8 of 10 milestones ahead of schedule
Team performed well	Team increased sales by 35% this quarter
Successfully launched campaign	Generated 2,500 qualified leads in first week
Improved customer satisfaction	Reduced complaint rate from 12% to 3%
Enhanced website performance	Cut page load time from 5s to 1.2s
Effective cost management	Reduced operating costs by $1M annually
Project moving forward nicely	All stakeholders signed off on phase 1
Positive training outcomes	90% of team now certified on new system

Check out Appendix B for enhancing your industry vocabulary

The Golden Rule: In business, you're not writing a novel but getting stuff done. So, keep it simple, clear, crisp and human. Precision shows you know your stuff and respect others' time. Whether you're emailing a client, or giving a presentation, aim for that verbal bullseye. Your ideas deserve it and your colleagues will thank you for it.

Strength Words

Strength words are all about lifting others and help individuals recognize the potential they might not see. When we use strength words to appreciate others, we go beyond simple compliments. We validate a person's inherent worth, recognize their unique qualities, boost their self-confidence and expand their self-concept.

Categorizing Strength Words

Personal Attributes

- **Emotional Intelligence**: Empathetic, Understanding, Receptive, Resourceful

- **Mental Agility**: Inquisitive, Progressive, Courageous, Open-minded, Direct
- **Character Strengths**: Genuine, Honest, Modest, Principled, Assured

Professional Competencies

- **Leadership Qualities**: Visionary, Commanding, Inspiring, Composed, Wise
- **Strategic Thinking**: Systematic, Judicious, Balanced, Innovative
- **Interpersonal**: Collaborative, Cooperative, Supportive, Diplomatic, Impartial
- **Adaptability**: Versatile, Spontaneous, Enterprising, Trend setter
- **Cognitive Processing**: Insightful, Illustrative, Comprehensive, Profound

Performance Indicators

- **Energy and Drive**: Unstoppable, Energetic, Alert, Purposeful, Resilient
- **Problem-Solving**: Analytical, Constructive, Trail-blazing, Creative
- **Approach to Challenges**: Resilient, Direct, Imaginative, Methodical

Instead of generic praise like "You're great," try:

- You're remarkably resilient in how you navigate challenges.
- Your empathy creates genuine connections with others.
- Your creativity brings innovative solutions to life.
- You don't just respond to change; you transform challenges into opportunities for growth.

- Your strategic thinking doesn't just solve problems, it anticipates and prevents them.
- Your ability to see multiple perspectives is a rare and valuable leadership skill.

Strength words are about seeing the unique light in each individual and helping them recognize their own brilliance.

Mastering Synonyms for Fluency

Synonyms are not just for impressing the English teacher. After all, a rich vocabulary isn't about impressing others; it's about expressing yourself with precision and flair.

Here's your rescue kit of power words that actually land in business:

Instead of "good," try:

- **For Products:** Efficient, User-Friendly, Robust
- **For Teams:** Collaborative, Dynamic, High-Performing
- **For Results:** Exceptional, Substantial, Impressive, Tangible, Desirable

Instead of "important," use:

- **For Deadlines:** Crucial, Vital, Essential
- **For Strategies:** Key, Fundamental, Critical
- **For Relationships:** Valuable, Significant, Pivotal

Quick power-ups for common business situations:

- **Talking Problems:** Challenges, Obstacles, Roadblocks
- **Showing Progress:** Advancing, Gaining Momentum, Moving Forward
- **Discussing Changes:** Transforming, Revamping, Optimizing

Team & Leadership Moves:

- **Work Together:** Collaborate, Partner, Team up, Join forces, Unite
- **Leadership:** Guidance, Mentoring, Stewardship, Coaching
- **Strategy:** Blueprint, Roadmap, Game Plan, Framework

Growth & Innovation Talk:

- **Growth:** Expansion, Advancement, Scaling, Flourishing
- **New:** Groundbreaking, Pioneering, Cutting-Edge, Revolutionary, Innovative
- **Make Better:** Improve, Enhance, Optimize, Elevate, Augment

Efficiency & Customer Focus:

- **Works Well:** Streamlined, Optimized, Resourceful, Proficient, Efficient, Effective
- **Helpful:** Customer-Focused, Client-Centric, User-Oriented, Service-Minded

The Antonym Advantage: Flip Your Message for Impact

Ever notice how sometimes saying what you don't want packs more punch than saying what you do? Here's a game-changer I learned from a senior exec: Instead of telling his team to "boost sales," he announced they were going to "eliminate missed opportunities." And he instantly got everyone's attention.

Try these power flips in your next meeting:

For Growth Talks:

- Increase efficiency → Eliminate waste
- Improve retention → Stop losing talent
- Boost productivity → Cut down idle time

For Customer Focus:

- Enhance satisfaction → Remove pain points
- Grow loyalty → Prevent customer churn
- Increase engagement → Eliminate frustration

For Team Dynamics:

- Build communication → Break down barriers
- Improve processes → Eliminate bottlenecks
- Accelerate progress → Prevent delays

In your next presentation, find one positive point and flip it. Watch how people react when you say "Let's stop losing deals" instead of "Let's win more deals." Sometimes the path to success is clearer when you spotlight what's in the way.

Pro Tip: Keep both versions in your back pocket. Some audiences need the positive spin, others need the wake-up call. Your job is to read the room and pick your punch.

Communication Impact Toolkit

Through years of navigating complex professional landscapes, I've discovered that words are more than just communication, they're strategic instruments of influence. This toolkit in Table 3.2 represents my hard-earned insights, distilled from countless meetings, negotiations, and transformative conversations where the right phrase made all the difference.

Adding Colour with Idioms and Phrases

I once watched my boss opened his board presentation with "Let's address the elephant in the room" about their market challenges, and suddenly everyone was all ears.

Table 3.2

Purpose	Alternative Phrases
Key Insights	• The bottom line: • Your North Star: • Make this your mantra: • The secret lies in: • What matters most: • The real power comes from:
What's missing	• Look closer: • Unlock this: • The real game-changer: • The breakthrough comes when: • The missing piece:
Revelation/Realization	• Let this sink in: • Reflect on this: • Ask yourself: • The mirror shows: • Your compass points to: • Question to ponder:
Inspiration/Motivation	• Let this fuel you: • Your power move: • Embrace this: • Your edge lies in: • Rise with this: • Your momentum starts here:
Transformation	• Your breakthrough waits in: • The shift happens when: • Your growth lies in: • The change starts with: • The pivot point is: • Your legacy builds on:

Here's your cheat sheet for phrases that actually work:

For Tough Conversations:

- **Cut to the chase** (get to the point without wasting time) *eg. Let's cut to the chase: we're 20% behind on Q4 targets!*
- **The ball in your court** (it's your turn to take action) *eg.* We've sent the proposal,the ball in your court for next steps.

- **Let's circle back** (return to discuss later) eg. *Let's circle back on the budget after the stakeholder meeting.*
- **Call a spade a spade** (speak honestly about something difficult) eg. *Let's call a spade a spade - this project needs a complete overhaul!*

For Team Motivation:

- **Hit the ground running** (start quickly and successfully) eg. *The new hires need to hit the ground running this January.*
- **Raise the bar** (set higher standards) eg. *Our competitor's launch means we need to raise the bar on quality.*
- **Get on the same page** (ensure everyone understands and agrees) eg.: *Before the client meeting, let's get on the same page about pricing.*
- **Go the extra mile** (make an extra special effort) eg. *The team went the extra mile to deliver before the deadline.*

For Strategic Talks:

- **Don't put all eggs in one basket** (avoid risking everything on a single venture) eg.: *We need to diversify our suppliers - can't put all eggs in one basket.*
- **Low-hanging fruit** (easy tasks with quick results) eg. *Let's tackle the website updates first - that's low-hanging fruit.*
- **Think outside the box** (approach problems creatively) eg. *This market needs something different - let's think outside the box.*
- **Get the ball rolling** (start something moving) → eg. *Let's get the ball rolling on the recruitment process.*

For Problem Solving:

- **Back to the drawing board** (start over from scratch) eg. *This design didn't pass user testing - back to the drawing board.*

- **Connect the dots** (understand the relationship between things) eg. *Once we connected the dots between customer complaints and the new UI...*
- **Kill two birds with one stone** (solve two problems with one action) eg. *This new software kills two birds with one stone: speeds up reporting and cuts costs.*
- **Break the ice** (get past initial awkwardness) eg. *Let's break the ice with a quick team introduction.*

For Project Management:

- **Keep the ball rolling** (maintain momentum) eg. *Great progress on phase one - let's keep the ball rolling into phase two.*
- **Pull your weight** (do your fair share of work) eg. *Every department needs to pull their weight to meet this deadline.*
- **Drop the ball** (fail to complete a task) eg. *Marketing dropped the ball on the social media campaign timing.*
- **In the pipeline** (in process of being developed or delivered) eg. *We have three major client contracts in the pipeline.*

For Negotiations:

- **Best of both worlds** (benefits of two different things) eg. *This hybrid work model gives us the best of both worlds.*
- **Bottom line** (the final, most important point) eg. *Bottom line: we need to increase prices by 10% to maintain margins.*
- **Meet halfway** (compromise equally) eg. *On the delivery timeline, we can meet halfway at four weeks.*
- **Seal the deal** (successfully complete an agreement) eg. *The* final presentation sealed the deal with the investors.

Check Appendix C for more, but master these first; they'll cover most of your business conversations.

At the end of the day, using idioms is all about reading the room. Throw them in at the right moment, and you can break the ice, drive your point home, or even save face in a tough situation. Just don't go overboard as nobody likes a show-off. Rather, use them wisely, and you'll be the talk of the water cooler in no time!

Emotional Intelligence in Language

Emotions in business? It used to be taboo. But times have changed, and for good reason.

Last week, a manager blasted his team for missing targets. Result? Two resignations.

Meanwhile, his senior handled the same situation with "*I know we're all feeling the pressure of these missed targets. Let's figure out how to get back on track together.*"

Result? Team rallied and crushed the next quarter.

It's not always easy. One manager shared how he told his team he was "disappointed" in their results. He quickly added, "*But I'm confident in our ability to turn this around.*" The mood shifted, opening the door to constructive problem-solving.

In business, people don't leave companies; they leave conversations that made them feel unheard.

Power Phrases That Build Trust:

- *I hear what you're saying about...*
- *I can understand how you feel...*
- *Help me understand...*
- *I appreciate you bringing this up...*
- *What are your thoughts on...*

Before any tough conversation, ask yourself: "*How would I want someone to tell this to me?*"

Business isn't just about spreadsheets and strategies - it's about people, we're all human, even in our work personas. Show genuine emotion, and watch how quickly "just another meeting" transforms into a meaningful connection. The secret? Keep it real, keep it relevant, but most importantly - keep it human.

Table 3.3

Situation	Harsh	Empathetic
Giving Feedback	Your presentation needs work	I'm excited about your ideas. Would you be open to some suggestions?
Managing Conflict	That's not what we agreed to	Help me understand your perspective
Client Issues	You can't resolve this client issue	I understand how important it's for you to resolve this. Here's what we can do...
Project Delay	Why isn't this done yet?	What obstacles are preventing us from completing this on time?
Team Performance	We're behind targets	I'm confident we can turn this around. What support do you need?
Change Management	This is the new policy, you need to adhere to	I know this change might feel challenging. Let's discuss your concerns
Crisis Communication	Some unforgivable mistakes were made	Let's take complete responsibility, and create a plan to fix it

Find your emotion-smart language playbook in Table 3.3.

Voice Modulation: Adding Depth to your Delivery

Voice modulation can make or break a presentation. Just ask Dinesh, a brilliant team leader who struggled to keep his team engaged during meetings. His monotone delivery had people checking their watches more often than their notes.

Before I give you some practical tips to enhance your vocal quality, I want you to understand this:

Your voice has three gears - use them appropriately:

- **Low gear:** Serious topics, bad news (slower, lower pitch that conveys authority)

- **Middle gear:** Daily conversations, updates (your normal voice for everyday discussions)
- **High gear:** Celebrations, motivational moments (more energy, higher pitch for captivating delivery)

Find some insights in Table 3.4 on various voice tools and how to use them effectively.

Table 3.4

Tool	Technique	Business Situation	Impact
Volume	Drop to just above a whisper	When making a crucial point	Forces everyone to lean in and listen
Pace	Slow down 20%	During complex explanations	Helps ideas sink in
Pitch	Slight rise at the end	When seeking input	Invites participation naturally
Pause	2-second silence	Before key numbers/ facts	Creates anticipation

Strategic Voice Deployment:

- **Meeting openings:** Start 10% louder
- **Difficult messages:** Lower pitch, slower pace
- **Team motivation:** Higher energy, faster pace
- **Questions:** Ending with upward inflection
- **Presentations:** Vary your pace and pitch
- **Critical feedback:** Use a measured and even tone

The bottom line is you're not doing a Shakespeare play, you're adding just enough variety to keep people's brains tuned in. Subtle variations create powerful engagement.

Navigating Diverse Communication Contexts

One size doesn't fit all in business communication. You wouldn't use the same language with a potential client as you would with your team during a casual brainstorming session.

I once saw a CEO switch from corporate speak to local slang when visiting a manufacturing plant. The workers loved it. It wasn't fake, it was a smart adaptation.

Ever watched someone bomb a presentation because they used tech jargon with non-tech executives? Or lose a client by being too casual. Let's fix that!

The 3-Second Context Check:
Before any business interaction, ask yourself:

- Who's my audience? (CEO, client, team member?)
- What's their communication style? (formal, casual, technical?)
- What do they need from this conversation? (information, motivation, decision?)

Power moves for different contexts are outlined in Table 3.5

Table 3.5

Context	Language Strategy	Communication Style
Board Room	Formal, Data-Driven	High-level strategic language
Team Huddle	Collaborative, Motivational	Conversational, goal-oriented
Client Interaction	Solution-Focused	Tailored to client's technical understanding
Technical Discussions	Precise, Detailed	Industry-specific language

Quick Adaptation Tricks:

- Mirror their pace (match fast or slow speakers)
- Match formality level (watch their word choices)
- Adapt to their technical knowledge (listen for industry terms they use)
- Follow their conversation style (do they prefer data or stories?)

The Key Principle: Consistent message with flexible delivery.

So, learn to listen more and adapt smartly. Your communication wardrobe should have versatile options.

The Power of Inquiry: Smart Questioning Techniques

For half of my life, I used to think being the smartest person in the room meant having all the answers. Until I realized that the real power lies in asking the right questions.

Last year, Rahul was stuck with a team that couldn't agree on anything. Instead of forcing decisions, he started asking: "What would make this a win for everyone?; Where do our goals actually overlap?; What's the worst that could happen if we tried X?" The mood shifted. People started listening to each other.

The QUEST Framework: Your Conversation GPS

Okay, this is gold - I wish I'd known about this years ago. It's called QUEST, and it's basically a cheat code for having amazing conversations.

- Quick opener: What brought you here today?/ What's top of mind for you?
- Unpack details: Tell me more about that challenge.../What is it about?
- Explore angles: How does this specifically impact you/How does this affect your team?
- Summarize understanding: So what I'm hearing is.../ Let me check if I understand...
- Transition forward: Where should we focus next?/ What's our best next step?

Power Moves That Actually Work:

Here's something they don't teach you in business school. Knowing when to shut up is just as important as knowing what to ask. Give people space. Let them think. Sometimes the most powerful question is followed by ten seconds of silence.

Refer to Table 3.6 for some power questions alternatives.

Table 3.6

Instead of Asking	Power Question Alternative	Strategic Value
Any questions?	What questions do you have?	Assumes engagement
Why did this fail?	What led to this outcome?	Non-threatening inquiry
Do you like it?	Which aspects resonate most?	Specific feedback
Are we on track?	What might get in our way?	Proactive problem-solving

Pro Tips:

- Replace "Why with What or How
- Allow silence after questions
- Use the phrase "Tell me more about..." or "What else"
- End meetings with "What haven't I asked about?"

Questions are your friends. Good ones open doors, spark ideas and sometimes save you from yourself. Bad ones... well, they teach you how to ask better questions next time.

And questions aren't about appearing smart, they're about getting smarter. The best ones are usually the simplest: "What do you mean by that?" has probably saved more deals than all the fancy business jargon in the world.

I've learned this stuff the hard way through countless meetings, pitches, and yes, a few facepalm moments. But hey, that's how we grow, right?

Chapter Wrap Up: Mastering Your Verbal Communication

Key Takeaways for Verbal Excellence

1. **Listen before you speak** Active listening isn't just hearing – it's understanding. When you truly listen, you respond with relevance and build deeper connections.
2. **Choose words with purpose** Your vocabulary isn't about impressing; it's about expressing. The right word at the right time can bridge understanding gaps and spark action.
3. **Master the modulation** Your voice is an instrument. Pitch, pace, and power work together to give your words the impact they deserve.
4. **Adapt and connect** Different contexts demand different approaches. The mark of a skilled communicator is the ability to shift styles while maintaining authenticity.
5. **Ask to understand** Questions are your compass in conversations. Smart inquiry builds engagement.

Your Verbal Communication Checklist

Before important conversations, remember:

- Are you listening to understand, not just to respond?
- Have you chosen words that clarify rather than complicate?
- Does your voice enhance your message?
- Is your style appropriate for the context?
- Are your questions opening doors to a deeper dialogue?

Great verbal communication isn't about perfection, it's about connection. When your words, voice, and listening skills work in harmony, you don't just speak; you engage, influence, and inspire.

CHAPTER 4

Constructing Clarity: Structuring Conversations with Ease

In business, clarity isn't just nice to have; it's the difference between being heard and being forgotten. A well-structured conversation is like a well-built bridge. It connects you to your audience seamlessly and guides your listeners from point A to point B.

In this chapter, you'll master the essential frameworks that make your messages stick. From crafting compelling openings to building strong arguments, you'll learn to structure your ideas so clearly that even complex messages become crystal clear.

The Power of Structured Communication

Two VPs pitched a million-dollar idea to their board.

- The first one "winged it" - brilliant points, but scattered everywhere.
- The second used a clear structure: Problem → Solution → Implementation → ROI.

Guess who got the funding?

When you take time to map out your message beforehand, meetings actually get somewhere instead of going in circles. You walk away with real decisions and the next steps, not just another meeting scheduled to discuss what you just discussed.

A manager decided to restructure his team's daily stand-ups:

- **Before**: 30-minute chaos of random updates
- **After**: 15-minute focused sessions using: Achievements, Roadblocks, and Next steps.

The Anatomy of a Conversation: Opening, Body, and Closing

Like any compelling narrative, a successful business conversation flows through three essential phases.

Opening: The Conversational Gateway

Think of your opening like the first few minutes of a good movie. It needs to grab attention and set direction. Use appropriate greetings and small talk to establish rapport.

- Hook attention: *Let me share something that might surprise you...*
- State purpose: *By the end of this discussion, we need to...*
- Set expectations: *This will take about 15 minutes...*

Your Power Openers:

1. Problem-Focused Openers:
    - *I noticed an interesting trend in our recent data...*
    - *Have you ever wondered why we keep facing this challenge?*
2. Solution-Oriented Openers:
    - *I found a way to reduce our processing time by X%...*
    - *Let me show you how we can streamline this process...*
3. Value-Adding Openers:
    - *I discovered a method that saved our department $X...*
    - *Here's something that could make your job easier, faster...*
4. Collaborative Openers:
    - *Could we brainstorm solutions for...*
    - *Let's explore how we might improve...*

5. Time-Sensitive Openers:
   - *Before we dive in, here's the key issue we need to address...*
   - *There's an urgent matter, I need your input on...*

The Body: Mapping Your Message

Start by acknowledging where you are ("Our retention rate is at 70%"), clearly state where you need to go ("Industry leaders maintain 90%"), then map out how to get there ("Here's our three-step plan to close this gap").

I once watched a Customer Manager saying: *"Team, our response time is currently 24 hours, we need to hit 4 hours to match our competitors, so let's walk through the specific changes we'll make to our support workflow to get there."*

Closing: The Art of Conclusion

The end of your conversation is what people tend to remember most. Yet it's often the most rushed part. A strong close doesn't need to be complicated. Simply remind people what was important and what happens next.

Power Closes that Work:

- Let's confirm three things... (For decisions)
- Your next steps are... (For delegating)
- What I'm understanding is... (For alignment)

Example: *So we've agreed on three things: [1,2,3]. Anand will handle X, Ekta will manage Y, and we'll review our progress next Friday. Does that capture everything?*

People rarely complain that a conversation was too clear or too well-organized. They do remember the ones that wandered or ended without clear direction.

Next time you have an important conversation ahead, take a moment to sketch these three parts. Your opening hook, your main points, your desired end state. Then let the conversation flow naturally within that framework.

Keep your Conversations Flowing & Connected

Ever watched a skilled leader transform a challenging meeting into a breakthrough discussion? They read the room like a book, pivot naturally when needed, and make everyone feel like their input matters.

Great communicators know when to push conversations forward and when to pause, keeping everyone interested without taking over. They also make sure everyone gets a chance to speak, involving quiet people while keeping louder voices in check.

Because at the end of the day, the best conversations aren't about perfect transitions, they're about perfect understanding.

Bridge Phrases That Actually Work:

- *This connects to our next point about...*
- *Now that we've covered X, let's explore Y...*
- *Before we move on, let's make sure we've captured...*
- *This reminds me of a similar situation where...*
- *Building on your point about...*

Pro Tips:

1. Every few minutes, loop back: *"Just to make sure we're aligned..."*
2. Use quick pulse checks: *"Does this resonate with your experience?"*
3. Before changing topics, confirm closure: *"Are we ready to shift gears?"*
4. When stuck, be human: *"Let's take a step back and make sure we're heading in the right direction."*
5. Reset if needed: *"Perhaps we should approach this from a different angle?"*

Common Professional Conversation Structures

PREP: Point, Reason, Example, Point

The PREP method is a versatile structure that helps you communicate your ideas clearly and persuasively.

- **Point:** Start by stating your main idea or argument concisely.
- **Reason:** Explain the logic behind your point. Why is this important? What evidence supports your stance?
- **Example:** Provide a specific, relevant example that illustrates your point and reason. This helps make your argument more concrete and relatable.
- **Point (Restated):** Conclude by restating your main point, reinforcing your message.

Example Application: In a product development meeting, you might use PREP to propose a new feature:

- *Integrate AI-powered customer service chatbots into our platform*
- *Reduce response times, improve satisfaction, lower costs*
- *Company X's results - 40% fewer tickets, 25% higher satisfaction in 3 months*
- *AI chatbots will boost both service efficiency and customer satisfaction*

Why-What-How: The Universal Clarifier

Here's how my client Alaina pitched a new customer service initiative:

- **Why:** *Our satisfaction scores dropped 15% this quarter, and we're losing customers to competitors with better service.*
- **What:** *So, we're launching a real-time feedback system for* customer calls.
- **How:** *Three-phase rollout: Install software next week, analyse first month's data, then scale to all teams by Q4.*

That's it - clean, clear, actionable. No rambling, no confusion, just the essence of what people need to know.

STAR (Situation, Task, Action, Result)

The STAR method is a powerful technique for structuring professional conversations, particularly when sharing experiences or answering behavioural interview questions.

Components of the STAR Method:

- **Situation**: Set the scene by providing context for your story
- **Task**: Explain the specific problem or goal you faced. Clarify your role and responsibilities in the situation.
- **Action**: Detail the steps you took to address the challenge. Focus on your personal contributions and decision-making process
- **Result**: Describe the results of your actions. Quantify the impact when possible. Reflect on lessons learned or skills gained

Example using the STAR Method:

- **Situation**: *Marketing and Sales teams had a strained relationship with Sales rejecting 60% of Marketing's leads as "not ready."*
- **Task**: *As Marketing Manager, I needed to create and implement a shared lead scoring system that both teams would use consistently.*
- **Action**: *Led joint team sessions, analysed 6-month lead data, created a 1–5 scoring framework, ran a two-week pilot program, and facilitated weekly feedback sessions to refine our criteria.*
- **Result**: *Increased lead acceptance rate to 85%, reduced sales cycle by 3 weeks, and saw our framework adopted by European offices as a best practice.*

AIDA (Attention, Interest, Desire, Action)

Basic Framework:

- **Attention**: Grab your audience's attention with a compelling hook
- **Interest**: Build interest by showing relevance to their needs
- **Desire**: Create desire by highlighting unique benefits and value
- **Action**: Drive action with a clear, compelling next step

Example:

- **Attention**: *We waste 12 hours weekly searching through different apps for project updates.*
- **Interest**: *Here's a single dashboard that saves teams 6+ hours* per week. Spotify and Nike already use it.
- **Desire**: *See all updates in one morning glance. Find any file in 2 clicks. Works with all your current tools.*
- **Action**: *Join Tuesday's 30-min demo at 10 AM. First 10 teams* get 3 months premium free. Click the link below to reserve your seat.

Problem-Solution-Benefit Structure

This structure is effective for persuasive communications, particularly in sales or when proposing new initiatives.

- **Problem:** Clearly articulate the challenge or pain point that needs to be addressed.
- **Solution:** Present your proposed solution, explaining how it directly addresses the identified problem.
- **Benefit:** Highlight tangible, measurable outcomes that will result from implementing your solution.

Example: In a client pitch for a consulting project, you might use this structure:

- **Problem**: *Your company's current supply chain model is leading to frequent stockouts and excessive inventory costs, impacting both customer satisfaction and profitability.*
- **Solution**: *We propose implementing a just-in-time inventory system coupled with predictive analytics to optimize your supply chain.*
- **Benefit**: *This solution will reduce your inventory costs by an estimated 30% and increase overall profitability by 15% within the first year of implementation.*

The key insight is that good conversations flow like a river, not a ping-pong match. Your job isn't to bounce from topic to topic but to guide the natural flow of ideas while making sure everyone's swimming in the same direction.

Tailoring Conversation Structure to Specific Purposes

Different business conversations require different frameworks. Here's how to structure each type from informative conversations to problem-solving conversations for maximum impact:

For some specific conversation structures, refer to Table 4.1:

Table 4.1

Purpose	Framework	Example
Informative Conversations	Headline → Key Points → Details	*Q1 sales exceeded targets by 15%. Three factors: new product launch, channel expansion, team restructuring.*
Persuasive Conversations	Problem → Impact → Solution → Benefits	*Current system creates 4-hour delays, costing $50K monthly.* *New software cuts delay to 30 minutes, saving $45K.*

Purpose	Framework	Example
Decision-Making Conversations	Options → Analysis → Recommendation	*Three vendor choices, all meeting criteria. Based on cost-benefit analysis, Vendor B optimal.*
Problem-Solving Conversations	Situation → Complication → Resolution	*Customer response time: 24 hours. Industry standard: 4 hours. Solution: automated first response.*

Real-World Conversation Scenarios and Structures

Each structure serves as a blueprint for guiding conversations toward specific outcomes while maintaining clarity and purpose.

For specific examples of conversations, refer to Table 4.2

Table 4.2

Scenario	Framework	Example Opening
Negotiation	Position → Interest → Options → Agreement	*Let's explore how we can create value for both organizations.*
Conflict Resolution	Situation → Perspectives → Common Ground → Solution	*I'd like to understand both viewpoints so we can find the best path forward.*
Client Consultation	Need → Challenge → Solution → Implementation	*Walk me through your current challenges so we can identify the best solution.*
Team Strategy	Current State → Goal → Barriers → Action Plan	*Let's align on where we are and where we need to go.*
Project Kickoff	Vision → Scope → Roles → Timeline	*Today we'll map out our path to successful delivery.*

Chapter Wrap Up: Looking Back, Moving Forward

Great conversations don't just happen, they're carefully crafted. Whether you're leading a team meeting or having a one-on-one, these techniques will help you create more meaningful and productive discussions.

- Clear opening sets direction, focused body delivers value and strong close drives action.
- Structure isn't rigid – it's your flexible framework for clarity.
- Every conversation needs a clear - What-Why-How.
- Different purposes need different frameworks.
- Listen as much as you speak and adapt your structure based on feedback.

Your Quick-Start Toolkit:

1. Before: Be clear about the purpose and map your 3 key points.
2. During: Use clear transitions and keep it flowing and connected.
3. After: Analyse what worked and what didn't work.

The Golden Rule: The best business conversations aren't the most elaborate, they're the ones that get the job done. Keep it clear, keep it purposeful, and keep it moving forward.

CHAPTER 5

The Power of Expression: Enhancing Your Verbal Artistry

Words can transform business realities in an instant. A demoralized sales force found their fire again after their manager smiled and said *"Revenue is down, but our comeback story starts today."* That's the power of words that make people think, feel, and act differently.

In this chapter, we'll stock your verbal paintbox with the tools that turn ordinary communication into compelling conversations that stick, inspire, and move people to action. No fancy jargon, complicated theories; just what works in real business contexts.

Painting with Words: Engaging the Listener's Imagination

Great business language isn't just heard - it's experienced. Are you ready to replace vague corporate speak with vivid images that stick?

Quick Wins for Different Situations:

For Meetings:

- Paint the big picture first: "*Imagine our customers walking into our stores and their faces lighting up like kids on Christmas morning* "
- Use contrast: "*Right now we're crawling. Next quarter? We'll be sprinting!*"
- Create mental snapshots: "*Picture your inbox completely* empty every Friday."

For Presentations:

- Open with a bang: "*Three years ago, we were working out of a garage. Today...*"
- Make data human: "*That's enough coffee cups to circle the* earth twice"
- Close with vision: "*This isn't just a product launch. It's a revolution in how people...*"

For Tough Conversations:

- Soften the blow: "*We're in the middle of a storm right now, but I see clear skies ahead*"
- Show empathy: "*I know this feels like climbing Everest in* flip-flops"
- Offer hope: "*This is just a chapter, not the whole story*"

You can see more such examples in Table 5.1.

Table 5.1

Communication Context	Purpose	Painted Version
Meetings & Updates	Revenue growth	*Our sales shot up like a rocket in July*
Presentations	Improved customer experience	*Every interaction feels like a first-class upgrade*
Strategy Sessions	Increasing competition	*We're in a street fight for market share*
Change Management	Facing challenges	*We're weathering a storm, but clear skies ahead*
Innovation Talks	Process improvement needed	*Time to break free from our rusty cage*
Team Success	Good collaboration	*We're moving like a well-oiled machine*

Create clarity through imagery, not poetry. Keep it sharp, keep it relevant, and always ask: "Can they imagine what I'm saying?"

Metaphors and Analogies: Bringing Ideas to Life

Technical jargons, complex processes, intricate concepts - these communication hurdles can kill great ideas before they take off. But what if you could turn any complicated idea into a simple story? That's where metaphors and analogies become your secret weapon.

Think of them as your universal translator in business. They turn complex ideas into instantly relatable concepts that stick in people's minds. Here's something I wish I had when I started out - a cheat sheet of metaphors that actually work in real business situations.

Table 5.2 provides a quick reference for metaphors for different business contexts.

Table 5.2

Business Concept	Metaphor	Example Usage
Market Strategy	Chess Game	While competitors make quick moves, we're positioning our pieces for a long-term advantage.
Change Management	Seasons	Like spring follows winter, this restructure brings new growth opportunities.
Team Leadership	Orchestra	Each department plays its unique part, but success comes from performing in harmony.
Innovation	Kitchen	Innovation is like creating a new recipe - experimenting, tasting, refining until perfect
Risk Management	Mountain Climbing	We've mapped the safest route, but we still need safety ropes for unexpected challenges.
Customer Relations	Gardening	Some clients flourish with light touch, others need intensive cultivation.
Program Management	Navigation	Clear destination, multiple routes, and we must adjust our course with changing winds.
Project Management	Wedding	This project is like planning a wedding - lots of moving parts, multiple stakeholders, and one date we can't miss.
Customer Journey	River Navigation	We're not just building bridges to customers; we're helping them navigate the entire stream

Business Concept	Metaphor	Example Usage
Brand Building	Architecture	Strong foundations first, then we build our brand skyward, floor by floor.
Data Security	Firewall	Think of our firewall like a bouncer at a club - checking IDs and keeping out trouble.

Pick metaphors that match your audience's interests. Sports analogies work great for some, cooking references for others. Read the room and adjust accordingly.

In my years of helping leaders grow, I've found that simple analogies speak louder than complex theories. When I share with an executive how looking for milk at a hardware store is like having wrong expectations from people, I see eyes their light up. These everyday examples have opened more minds and touched more hearts than any complex leadership model.

- **Living in an Echo Chamber** - Surrounding yourself only with people who share your views is like standing in a room full of mirrors. You keep seeing reflections of your own thoughts, never experiencing the full spectrum of perspectives that exists outside.
- **The Time Traveler's Photo Album** - Dwelling on past mistakes is like flipping through a photo album where you've only kept the blurry, poorly-lit pictures. You're missing all the beautiful moments that tell the complete story of your life.
- **The Rearview Mirror** - Living in the past is like trying to drive forward while only looking in the rearview mirror - you'll keep crashing into what's ahead.
- **The Dirty Window** - Negative thinking is like looking through a dirty window - everything you see is clouded by the dirt, not because the world is actually dark.
- **The Weight Training** - Carrying grudges is like doing everyday tasks while wearing ankle weights. You can still move

forward, but everything becomes unnecessarily harder, and you're the only one feeling the burden.

The Emergency Cheat Sheet

When you need a quick metaphor for:

- Change → Weather/Seasons/Tides
- Growth → Garden/Seeds/Roots
- Strategy → Journey/Navigation/Chess
- Competition → Sports/Games/Racing
- Innovation → Cooking/Building/Art & Science

The Golden Rule: The best metaphors aren't the most clever - they're the ones that make people say "Oh, now I get it!" These are tools, not tricks. Use them to illuminate, not decorate.

The Art of Storytelling: Engaging Hearts and Minds

Two CEOs at a leadership summit presented their company's digital transformation journey. The first showed slides packed with data. The second started with, *"Three years ago, I made a decision that almost cost us everything..."*

Guess which one caught instant attention?

That's the magic of the story. And it's not just magic – it's science.

Why Stories Hijack Our Brains (In a Good Way)

When you deliver quarterly numbers, people nod politely. But tell them about the junior engineer who spotted a small issue that saved the company millions, everyone leans forward. While facts stream through our short-term memory, stories trigger dopamine and emotionally charged memories that stick.

Our brains are wired for stories. When someone says, "*Let me tell you about the time when...*", your neural pathways light up like Times Square.

Stories vs. Anecdotes: Choosing the Right Tool

The fancy new coffee machine broke. The team found the old machine in storage. Turned out it made better coffee. A quick lesson about complex not always is a better option.

A failing restaurant turned around when the owner started asking each employee to write one customer interaction in a diary each day. No complaints or sales - just moments. Three months later, that book became their training manual, menu inspiration, and even drew customers who'd heard about "the place that collects stories." They'd discovered their brand wasn't about food - it was about gathering human moments.

See the difference? The first one is an anecdote and the second one a story.

Anecdotes are quick jabs that make one point. Stories are journeys that change minds! Find detailed comparison of stories and anecdotes in Table 5.3:

Table 5.3

Element	Stories	Anecdotes
Purpose	Drive deep change and create lasting impact through emotional connection	Make quick points and create immediate relatability through shared experiences
Structure	Full narrative arc with conflict, challenge, and resolution	Single moment or incident that illustrates a specific point
Time	2–3 minutes, multiple scenes and characters	30 seconds max, focused on one moment
Impact	Transforms thinking and inspires action	Breaks ice or reinforces a point
Best For	• Strategic presentations • Vision sharing • Change management • Team inspiration	• Meeting ice-breakers • Quick examples • Lightening the mood • Transition moments
Result	Long-term mindset shifts and behavioural change	Immediate understanding or quick laugh

Think of stories as your strategic weapons and anecdotes as your tactical tools. Choose based on your goal and available time.

Storytelling Strategies for Leaders

Picture two leaders giving updates about a troubled project:

The first stands up, slides polished to perfection: "*We encountered obstacles but persevered through strategic pivoting...*"

The second takes a different approach: "*Last Tuesday, I walked into our team meeting and saw the exhaustion in everyone's eyes. Our biggest client was threatening to walk. That's when we realized we had to completely rethink our approach...*"

Which one would you remember?

Every great leader can become an enthralling storyteller. Not by mastering fancy techniques, but by learning to share their truth in ways that move people to action. So, find your moments of truth to find your stories.

- What crisis taught you most?
- Which failure changed everything?
- What success made you feel proud?

Crafting Compelling Narratives

The best business stories are not complex. They're human. Like the origin story of how a coffee stain on a designer's desk led to their most successful product feature.

✗ *Our new customer strategy emphasizes deeper market penetration.*

✓ *In my first sales job, I learned that every 'no' teaches you something about your 'yes.' That insight is driving our new approach: we're talking to every customer who left us last year to build something better.*

Your Story Framework

1. Before: Set the scene with specific details
2. Trigger: Name the moment everything changed
3. Action: Share the human response, not just the business strategy
4. Result: Show both the practical and emotional impact
5. Learning: Connect it to today's challenge

Making Your Stories Work

Look for the moment that made you feel something - that's where your story should begin. The numbers can come later; start with the scene that mattered.

- **Drop into the Action** *The client closed his laptop mid-presentation and said, 'This isn't what we asked for'*
- **Make It Human** *At 8 PM, while ordering our third round of* pizza, Alex pulled up another chair and said, 'Let's solve this together!'
- **Raise the Stakes** *If we didn't fix this bug by morning, 10,000* users would wake up to frozen screens.
- **Show, Don't Tell** *In three different meetings, I heard three different versions of the same project plan.*
- **Create Contrast** *Two weeks later, that same client was introducing us to his entire network.*

The One Rule that Matters the Most

Be real. Your team doesn't need you to be perfect. They need you to be human.

Your mistakes, doubts, and struggles aren't weaknesses in your story - they're the parts that make people trust you.

The **Strategic Storytelling** framework is outlined in Table 5.4

Table 5.4

Story Type	Purpose	Structure	Example
Origin Story	Build Connection	Challenge → Idea → Transformation	*We started in a small room with three laptops and a coffee machine...*
Human Story	Build Trust	Vulnerability → Learning → Growth	*My biggest mistake as a leader taught me...*
Crisis Story	Show Values	Problem → Choice → Impact	*When our biggest client threatened to leave, we chose integrity over profit...*
Vision Story	Inspire Action	Present Pain → Future Possibility → Path	*Imagine walking into our office five years from now...*
Innovation Story	Drive Change	Frustration → Solution → Results	*One developer's mistake became our best-selling feature...*
Customer Journey	Create Empathy	Challenge → Discovery → Success	*Amma almost gave up until she found our solution...*
Breakthrough Story	Inspire Persistence	Setback → Pivot → Achievement	*After five failed attempts, we finally cracked the code...*
Transformation Story	Enable Change	Old Way → Catalyst → New Reality	*We thought remote work would break us. Instead, it made us stronger...*

People don't buy logic. They buy stories with clear next steps.

Pro Tips:

- Match story type to audience need
- Keep it short and focused
- End with clear takeaway
- Use real details, not fluff
- Practice the opening line

Examples from the Corporate World:

The Origin Story That Changed Everything

"We couldn't make rent. We had three air mattresses and a crazy idea..."

Simple, desperate, human. That's how Airbnb introduces their origin story. It works because who hasn't struggled with bills? When they reveal how they transformed from anxious renters to global disruptors, it's so inspiring and relatable.

The Vision Story That Inspired Action

"Imagine never stopping for gas again. Your car gets better while you sleep."

Tesla didn't sell electric cars – they sold the future. By focusing on what's possible (never refueling) rather than what's technical (battery capacity), they turned sceptics into believers and made the impossible feel inevitable.

The Culture Story That Transformed Service

"We offer new employees $2,000 to quit."

With one counterintuitive move, Zappos tells you everything about their culture. They'd rather pay people to leave than keep those who aren't all in. It's memorable because it's bold, specific, and puts real money behind their values.

Details make the story real, emotions make it memorable, and honesty makes it powerful. When done right, your story becomes their story. And that's when real change happens.

Harnessing the Power of Quotes: Inspiring Through Words

You've seen it happen. Someone drops the perfect quote in a meeting, and suddenly the energy shifts.

Why Quotes Pack a Punch

Think of quotes as concentrated wisdom - like espresso shots for the mind. They work because they:

- Borrow authority (Einstein tends to be more convincing than Bob from accounting)
- Package complex ideas simply ("Just do it" vs. a 50-page strategy document)
- Create shared reference points ("Remember what Steve Jobs said about...")

Choosing Quotes That Actually Work

Skip: The Pinterest wisdom ("Live, Laugh, Love"

Use:

- Unexpected wisdom ("The best way to predict the future is to create it")
- Industry-specific insights ("Design is not just what it looks like. Design is how it works")
- Contextual relevance ("The best time to plant a tree was 20 years ago. The second best time is now")

Making Quotes Land in Real Situations

The difference between a quote that falls flat and one that changes minds lies not in the words themselves, but in knowing exactly when to use them, as these battle-tested examples show:

- **On Change:** *"Change is hard at first, messy in the middle, and gorgeous at the end."* -Robin Sharma
- **On Persistence:** "*It's not whether you get knocked down, it's whether you get up.*" -Vince Lombardi
- **On Authenticity:** **"***Be yourself; everyone has already been taken***."** -Oscar Wilde
- **On Innovation:** *"Innovation is saying no to 1,000 things."* - Steve Jobs
- **On Visionary Thinking:** *"If I had asked people what they wanted, they would have said faster horses."* -Henry *Ford*
- **On Transformation:** *"The cave you fear to enter holds the treasure you seek."* -Joseph Campbell

Creating Your Own Quotable Moments

The best quotes? They're not always from famous people. They come from real leaders in real moments.

Transform:

- "We need to innovate more"
  Into: "Yesterday's solutions won't solve tomorrow's problems"
- "Customer service matters"
  Into: "Every phone ring is a chance to write our story"

The setup matters: Don't just drop quotes. Give context that makes them relevant, connecting them to your current situation

Instead of "As Winston Churchill said..." **Try:** "This reminds me of what Churchill faced in 1940..."

Your best quotes will come from:

- Crisis moments ("This isn't a setback, it's our comeback story")
- Vision casting ("We're not building features, we're building futures")
- Culture building ("We don't avoid problems, we collect solutions")

Your Quote Bank Strategy

Keep three types ready:

1. **Universal** (Change, Leadership, Innovation)
2. **Industry-specific** (From pioneers and thought leaders)
3. **Personal** (Your own hard-won insights)

The best quote isn't the one that sounds smartest - it's the one that makes people think, "I needed to hear that.

The Art of Business Humour: When to Crack a Smile

Great leaders know humour isn't about being funny - it's about being human.

When Netflix's service crashed, they tweeted: "We're sorry for the inconvenience. Maybe it's time to go outside and build a snowman?" They acknowledged the problem, stayed on brand, and made people smile.

Smart humour can break the tension in tough moments and make difficult topics approachable.

What Works (And What Doesn't)

Green Light Humour:

- Self-deprecating: *After my first quarterly presentation, PowerPoint and I needed couples counselling.*
- Shared experiences: *Our strategic plan is so ambitious, my coffee maker just asked for a raise.*
- Universal frustrations: *Our printer has only two moods: 'Not now' and 'Really not now.'*

Red Light Humor:

- Project mismanagement: *This project plan was clearly written by a random word generator.*
- Office politics: *Upper management's decision-making speed rivals continental drift.*
- Personal Critiques: *Marketing's strategy is like their fashion sense...*
- Client criticism: *Client X's feedback is as clear as mud*
- Office gossips: *The office power couple spends more time planning their coffee break than we spend on quarterly strategy*

Business humour isn't about being funny; it's about using the right light touch at the right moment, as these field-tested examples show.

Change Management Moments

- *We're not lost, we're just taking the scenic route to our objectives.*
- *Our org chart has changed so much, even my coffee mug needs a new reporting structure.*
- *Think of this restructure like a software update - there might be bugs, but we'll all work better afterward.*

Technical Difficulties

- *Our system is experiencing an unscheduled meditation session.*
- *The servers are having their own version of a Monday morning.*
- *Our network is moving at the speed of a committee decision.*

Tough Deadlines

- *This timeline is like my diet - ambitious but technically possible.*
- *Our deadline is so tight, my calendar just filed for overtime.*
- *We're not behind schedule - we're building anticipation.*

Project Challenges

- *Our budget is like my smartphone battery - we need to be strategic about usage.*
- *This project has more phases than my teenage fashion choices.*
- *We've hit so many pivots, we could qualify for the Olympic gymnastics team.*

Meeting Moments

- *If this meeting were a movie, we'd be in the part where the hero faces their biggest challenge.*
- *I've been in so many Zoom calls, my kids think I work for a webcam company.*
- *Let's make this meeting like a good sandwich - meaty in the middle, brief on the ends!*

Pro Tips:

1. Read the room (What works in start-ups might bomb in banking)
2. When in doubt, leave it out
3. Self-deprecation over criticism
4. Keep it light and professional
5. Time it right - humour during a crisis needs extra sensitivity
6. Cultural awareness - what's funny in one region might not translate globally
7. Follow the "punch up" rule - joke about situations, not individuals
8. Build rapport first - humour lands better when there's trust
9. Less is more - one well-timed quip beats a string of jokes

If a joke falls flat, acknowledge it lightly and move on. "*Well, that was as successful as my first try at baking bread - let's get back to work!*"

The Golden Rule: Business humour should build bridges, not burn them. When used skillfully, it can transform tense situations into teachable moments and strengthen team bonds.

Chapter Wrap Up: The Art of the Moment

Simple formula for any important message:

1. Open with a story that hooks
2. Use a metaphor that clarifies
3. Reinforce with a powerful quote
4. Lighten with appropriate humour
5. Close with a clear image of tomorrow

Example in action: *"Six months ago, our innovation lab was quieter than a library during finals (metaphor). We had more failed experiments than Edison's light bulb attempts (story). As Einstein said, 'Imagination is more important than knowledge' (quote). And trust me, some of our early prototypes looked like they were designed in the dark (humour). Today, we're not just turning on lights - we're illuminating industries (vision)."*

The Golden Rule: The goal isn't to sound eloquent. It's to be understood, remembered and acted upon.

The best expression feels natural, serves the message, and moves people forward. Whether you're using stories, metaphors, quotes, or humour, always ask: "Does this make my message clearer and more compelling?"

Chapter 6

Sailing Smoothly, Communicating with Cultural Sensitivity

In today's global business landscape, business transcends borders that makes it essential to be mindful of cultural sensitivities and norms. Working across cultures is about reading the room and adjusting how you communicate with people from different backgrounds. Think of it like learning the unwritten rules of a new group - each culture has its own way of building trust and getting things done.

This chapter shows you how to navigate these differences naturally. You'll learn to pick up on subtle cues, like why your Japanese colleague pauses before responding, or why your Thai teammate might agree with you even when they have concerns. These practical tips will help you build genuine connections with people from any culture, making your global work relationships smoother and more effective.

Cultural Awareness in Global Business

You know that moment when you realize cultural understanding isn't just about East vs. West? Priya, a tech leader was brilliant at getting her US team to understand Indian communication styles, but here's what surprised her - she needed different approaches for her Japanese and Korean teams, even though they're both Asian!

Let me tell you about the "meeting before the meeting" phenomenon. Raj, a senior manager at a major IT firm, was frustrated that his German colleagues seemed to make all decisions before the official meetings. Meanwhile, his German counterpart couldn't understand why important discussions in India often happened over *chai* breaks.

Here's a game-changer insight from Anita, who leads operations for a tech giant: "In India, we're natural code-switchers. We already changed our communication style between family, office, and clients. Global business just adds more switches."

The best part? Our Indian business culture has some built-in advantages for global communication. That inherent respect for hierarchy helps when dealing with Japanese firms.And our adaptability? Gold in today's global business world!

The Iceberg Model of Culture

Think of culture like an iceberg floating in the ocean. What we see above the water is just the tip that represents the visible aspects of workplace culture that are easy to spot on your first day. But the real force, the mass that shapes everything above, lies beneath the surface.

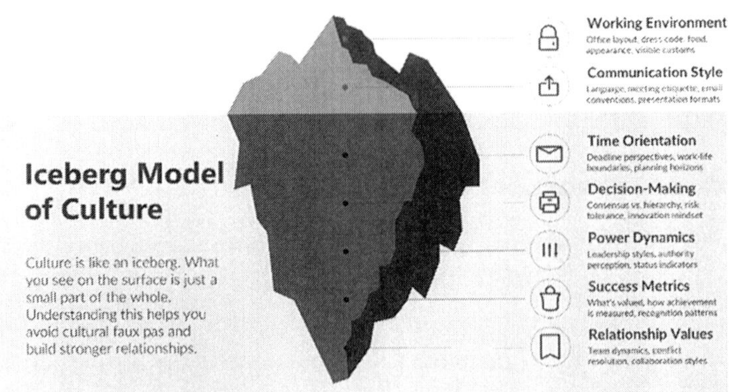

Developing Cultural Quotient (CQ)

What's CQ Really About? Think of it like upgrading your social operating system for the global stage. It's that sixth sense that helps you navigate different cultural waters without sinking. You must understand the invisible currents that guide how different people think, decide, and build trust.

Here's how CQ works:

- **Drive**: It's your cultural curiosity and confidence. It's about being comfortable with being uncomfortable. You need that inner engine pushing you to understand and acclimatize.
- **Knowledge**: Not just textbook stuff, but real understanding of how cultures tick differently like it's about knowing why your German clients need everything in writing.
- **Strategy**: This is your cultural GPS - planning how to navigate different cultural territories. Think of it as your "if-then" cultural playbook.
- **Adaptation**: Here's where theory meets reality - actually adjusting your style while staying authentic. It's like being a cultural chameleon without losing your true colours.

Meera was frustrated about working with her global team. "I've read all the books about cultural differences but something's still off", she told me over coffee.

Think of cultural intelligence like learning to dance. You can study all the steps, but until you get on the floor and feel the rhythm, you're not really dancing. Meera's breakthrough? She stopped trying to memorize "cultural rules" and started getting curious about her team's stories. I love how she put it: "I stopped being a cultural tourist and became a cultural explorer."

It starts with genuine curiosity - what I call "coffee conversations." One of my clients turned his team's fortune around simply by starting every call with "Tell me something interesting from your world." His Swedish team member shared about their coffee breaks (fika), which led to a whole new understanding of work-life balance.

Another client, a sales director keeps what she calls her "cultural curiosity journal" - little observations about how her global clients react to different approaches.

Had this client who thought she needed to act "more American" with her US team. Her breakthrough came when she realized cultural intelligence is about building bridges while staying authentic.

Growing Your CQ:

1. Get Curious: Start with genuine interest in different ways of doing things.
2. Observe Patterns: Notice how different cultures handle the same situation.
3. Practice Flexing: Try different approaches based on your cultural context.
4. Learn from Mistakes: Every cultural misstep is actually a learning goldmine.

Start small, stay curious, and remember - perfect cultural intelligence doesn't exist. What exists is the constant journey of learning and adapting!

Had this brilliant Indian tech leader who kept failing with European clients until she started using what she called her "cultural pause button" - taking a moment to think "How might they see this?" before every interaction.

Common Cultural Differences

Cultural differences significantly impact global business interactions. Here are key areas where cultures diverge:

Direct vs. Indirect Communication

Those subtle hints we Indians drop to avoid saying "no" directly? They fly right over American heads. A tech VP learned to say "We have some concerns about this timeline" instead of "We'll do our best." Do be more explicit with Western teams while staying polite.

High-Context vs. Low-Context

Our Indian style of building full context before getting to the point often frustrates American clients who want the headline first. A team lead now starts with the conclusion, then adds context. Do lead with key points for Western audiences, save the background for follow-up.

Individualism vs. Collectivism

When that US client keeps pushing for "who exactly did this great work?" while we're trying to highlight team effort? A marketing manager now balances it: "Priya led this initiative, supported by our exceptional team." Do acknowledge individual contributions while maintaining team harmony.

Long-term vs. Short-term Orientation

Our Indian tendency to build lasting relationships before business can test American partners who expect quick deals. A consultant now blends approaches: quick initial wins while building deeper connections. Do respect Western quarterly pressures while nurturing long-term bonds.

Work-life Balance Expectations

That 9 PM call we think is normal? It's a big no-no for European colleagues. An IT director learned to schedule calls within common working hours, even if it meant starting his day earlier. Do respect strict work-life boundaries, especially with European teams.

Non-Verbal Communication

That slight head wobble we Indians do? It can really confuse Western colleagues. A senior executive from Delhi learned to pause it during global video calls after his US teammates kept asking, "Is that a yes or no?" Do maintain steady eye contact in Western meetings, but remember to soften it in East Asian contexts.

Time Orientation

Forget "Indian Stretchable Time" when dealing with German or Swiss clients - they see time as money, literally. An IT firm lost a major contract because they thought "EOD" meant "end of their day" rather than German time. Do set clear time zones and deadlines in writing. "5 minutes" doesn't mean 15 in Switzerland! An Indian IT firm now adds buffer time in their schedules with German clients. Do respect exact timing with Western partners - they see it as basic professionalism.

Power Distance

That comfortable close distance we maintain during conversations? Pulls Western clients right out of their comfort zone. A Delhi sales team now stands an arm's length away during international meetings. Do respect the bigger personal bubble in Western cultures.

Just because your Swedish colleague insists on first names doesn't mean you should do the same in Singapore. A Mumbai team leader nailed it by using titles in formal meetings but switching to first names in one-on-ones. Do mirror your client's formality level rather than imposing your comfort zone.

Decision-Making

Our Indian consensus-building approach can test American clients' patience. One Pune tech company solved this by having quick initial alignments before longer group discussions. Do give clear timelines for when decisions will be made, especially with Western partners.

Risk Tolerance

Our 'jugaad' mindset can terrify German partners who want everything planned to the last detail. A Noida startup now creates detailed risk assessments for European clients while keeping it flexible with Southeast Asian partners. Do match your partner's planning intensity. Those detailed contracts Germans insist on? They're not questioning your integrity - it's their business culture. A Hyderabad startup now prepares micro-detailed proposals for European clients while keeping it broader for Southeast Asian partners. Do match your documentation level to your client's culture.

Navigating Business Etiquette Across Cultures

Understanding variations in business etiquette is crucial for successful international interactions. Watch a seasoned global leader work: Each gesture, timing choice, and conversation rhythm shifts subtly as they move from a Berlin boardroom to a Mumbai office to a negotiation in Germany.

Greetings & Introductions: That firm handshake you practiced? Dial it down in Japan! Do lead with a slight bow in East Asia, stick to *namaste* in doubt. One of my clients now brilliantly starts with "How do you prefer to greet in your culture?"

Business Cards: Our casual "pocket it quickly" approach? Big mistake in Japan and Korea. Do receive cards with both hands in Asian countries and check them out respectfully.

Meeting Protocol: Remember, not every culture loves our Indian "jump straight into shop talk" style. A Delhi team now starts Korean meetings with light personal chat about family, weather. Do mirror your host's pace - some cultures need three cups of tea before talking numbers.

Also, our tendency to have multiple parallel discussions in meetings can overwhelm Western colleagues. Do stick to one speaker at a time in Western meetings.

Gift-Giving: That expensive Diwali gift box could get your US partner in serious trouble with compliance. Do keep corporate gifts small and symbolic with Western companies. One of my clients swears by Indian handicrafts, unique but not too valuable.

Dining Etiquette: Our "try everything to please the host" approach works great in China but can backfire in Western settings where finishing everything might not be expected. Do check if your host drinks alcohol before ordering wine.

Negotiation Styles Our Indian love for relationship-building over tea can test American partners' patience. A clever Noida CEO now says "Let's have a quick informal chat before our official meeting." Do adapt your pace - fast with US, slower with the Middle East.

Dress Code That super casual Silicon Valley style doesn't work in Tokyo. Do err on the formal side until you understand local norms.

Communication Channels Not everyone loves our WhatsApp business culture! Learn to stick to email with German clients. Do check preferred communication platforms - WeChat for China, Line for Japan, and email for Europe.

Office Hierarchy Our respect for age and position? Can confuse Scandinavian partners who expect everyone to speak up.

Keep a "culture cheat sheet" for each major partner country. But remember that these aren't rigid rules. As my mentor says, "Let authenticity lead, and cultural awareness guide your interactions!"

What They Say vs. What They Mean

Table 6.1 includes some head-scratching phrases we often encounter in global business - especially useful from an Indian context!

Table 6.1

Phrase	Cultural Meaning	Real Example
Let's discuss offline	US/UK: Need private chat India: Topic closed	Indian team missed important 1:1 meeting, thinking US client wanted to drop the topic
Interesting...	UK: Dislike US: Genuinely interested Germany: Need data	Bangalore startup misread British investor's polite rejection
Soon	Germany: 24 hours India: Flexible Middle East: Inshallah	German client expected next-day delivery when Indian team meant "eventually"
Maybe	Japan: No India: Possible US: Probably yes	Mumbai team kept waiting for Japanese partner's approval after a clear "no"

Phrase	Cultural Meaning	Real Example
That's challenging	UK: Impossible India: We'll try Germany: Problem to solve	Chennai team missed UK client's rejection of timeline
I'll try my best	Japan: Yes India: Might not happen US: Will make effort	US client expected his vendor to update progress

Quick Tips for Major Business Cultures

Cultural intelligence opens doors that perfect PowerPoints can't.

Table 6.2 below provides some actionable tips for different cultures.

Culture	Key Strategy	Proven Win
US	Start with "30-second version" - expand only if asked	Mumbai firm won $2M deal by respecting time boundaries
Japanese	Schedule 15min pre-meeting chat, focus on relationships	Bangalore startup turned $500K deal into $1.2M
German	Send detailed agendas 48hrs ahead, stick to timelines	Indian IT firm secured 3-year partnership by maintaining precision
Chinese	Build relationship first, decisions follow	6-month relationship building led to $12M contract
British	Listen for tone over words, document subtle cues	Delhi firm increased UK clients by 40% using tone-based approach
Middle Eastern	Dedicate first 30min to personal connection	Gulf partnership led to 5-year exclusive distribution rights

These aren't rigid rules - they're starting points. Let these guide you, but let the person in front of you teach you!

Power Questions That Build Trust

- Help me understand your priorities.
- What does success mean to you?
- How would you prefer to handle this?

Trust Builders by Region

- US/UK: Clear contracts, met deadlines
- Asia: Long-term relationships, shared meals
- Middle East: Personal connections first
- Europe: Structured processes, precision
- Germany: Technical excellence, punctuality
- Japan: Group consensus, patient listening

Keep interaction style aligned with local trust markers - contracts in US, relationships in Asia, process in Europe.

Navigating Cross-Cultural Business Interactions

Here are some real life scripts that you might find helpful. **Building Initial Connection** "I'd love to learn about your organization before we begin."

- US: "What are your priorities for Project X?"
- Asia: "Your company's growth is impressive - tell me more?"
- Europe: "Shall we share our industry backgrounds?"

Starting Negotiations "Let's explore mutual value creation."

- Germans: "I have a detailed proposal. Shall we review it properly?"
- Chinese: "How do you see this partnership evolving?"
- Middle East: "What's your ideal vision for this partnership?"

Managing Disagreements "Could we explore different perspectives?"

- Japan: "May I share an alternative view?"
- US: "I have concerns about X. Thoughts?"
- Nordics: "Let's align based on the data."

Follow-ups "About our discussion on X - confirming next steps."

- UK: "Would a summary of key points help?"
- Korea: "Have I captured everything correctly?"
- France: "Shall we schedule time to explore further?"

Remember to adapt these to your style and context.

Overcoming Cultural Barriers: Managing Cultural Biases

If you are ready to recognize your cultural blind spots, let me share something about cultural biases - they're like your phone's background apps, running without you noticing. I see this all the time coaching global teams. We assume our way is the "normal" way; we judge others through our cultural lens; we mistake differences for deficiencies.

Key Mindset Shifts:

- Replace "that's strange" with "that's different"
- Ask "what makes this logical?" not "why are they difficult?"
- Remember: Different doesn't mean wrong

Practical Tools:

1. Power Pause: Take 5 seconds before reacting to unexpected responses
2. Context Question: "What would make this approach make perfect sense?"

Real Example: German team's detailed documentation requests isn't distrust but cultural value of precision and clarity

This shift helps avoid misreading normal cultural differences as problems. Practice pausing to understand context before judging.

Cross-Cultural Integration Case Study

Situation: Global tech merger with leaders from Mumbai, New York, China, and Sweden. 6-month IT integration deadline.

Challenges:

- Mumbai style: Relationship-focused, flexible timelines
- New York style: Direct, time-driven
- Chinese approach: Hierarchical, consensus-based
- Swedish method: Collaborative, balanced

Solution:
"3-Zone Meeting" framework:

1. Green: Build relationships
2. Yellow: Status updates
3. Red: Decision-making

Key Tools:

- Clear communication guide ("maybe" = no)
- Designated collaboration hours
- 24-hour email response window

Results:

- Early project completion
- Leveraged strengths:
    - New York: Urgent decisions
    - Mumbai: Stakeholder relations
    - China: Quality control
    - Sweden: Team alignment

Chapter Wrap Up: Your Cultural Navigation Toolkit

In global business, understanding different cultures matters more than any business plan.

Key Moves for Global Business

1. Listen for unsaid messages - silence can mean "no" in Tokyo
2. Match trust styles - US values contracts, China builds bonds over meals, Germany relies on detailed plans
3. Open with connection - "What's interesting in your world?"
4. Read body language - crossed arms and tone shifts signal issues
5. Show cultural curiosity - "How would this work in your culture?"
6. Ask more, judge less - "Tell me more about that"
7. Stay authentic with awareness - adapt without losing yourself.

Cultural Navigation Tools

- Observe behaviors and styles
- Adjust approach by location
- Lead with curiosity over perfection

Daily Habits

- Before global meetings, ask: "What might they need that's different?"
- After each interaction, note one cultural insight
- When uncertain, choose curiosity over certainty

Stop trying to be a cultural expert. Start being a cultural explorer. Your mistakes, handled with humility and curiosity, often build more trust than your successes.

Afterall you're not changing who you are - you're expanding who you can be.

CHAPTER 7

Poise Under Pressure: Managing Difficult Conversations

You know those conversations that make your stomach churn. Whether it's telling a star performer they didn't get the promotion, navigating a delicate negotiation, or navigating a heated conflict - these moments can feel like walking through a minefield.

In this chapter, we'll explore how to transform these daunting dialogues into diplomatic masterpieces. Not by avoiding hard truths, but by delivering them in ways that maintain dignity, build respect, and drive positive change. Because in today's complex business world, we're all diplomats, whether we realize it or not.

The Art of Diplomatic Communication

First, let's ditch this idea that being diplomatic means being fake or manipulative. My most successful clients aren't the ones who sugar-coat anything; they're the ones who've mastered what I call "compassionate clarity."

Think of it like being a doctor delivering tough news. You don't want a doctor who beats around the bush about a serious condition, but you also don't want one who blurts it out without empathy.

Diplomacy is how deeply you understand the human dynamic at play. It's about feeling the undercurrents, and choosing your approach accordingly. Think of it as emotional intelligence meeting strategic thinking over coffee.

In today's complex business world, this skill isn't just nice to have - it's essential for survival as your ability to be diplomatically direct could make or break crucial relationships.

At its heart, effective diplomacy begins with the right mindset and with genuine care. Before entering any conversation, ask yourself: "What do I want for this person?"

As CXO clients says, "I used to see difficult conversations as problems to solve. Now I see them as bridges to build." And that's what separates good leaders from great ones in these moments!

Key Principles of Business Diplomacy

Let me break these down from years of watching leaders navigate tricky business waters - no fluff, just real insights. Think of these as your diplomatic survival kit:

The Power of Intention: A senior leader transformed a tense performance discussion by opening with "I want to ensure you succeed here" instead of listing failures.

Respect for All Parties: It's not just about being polite - it's about genuinely valuing different perspectives. Each of us sees this situation through a different lens, and that's actually valuable.

Emotional Intelligence: Read the room, feel the vibe. It's about catching those unspoken signals, the crossed arms, the subtle shift in tone. A Mumbai executive says, "Watch faces, not just spreadsheets."

Listen to understand deeply, not to respond. When people feel heard, their defences drop. A Chennai team leader transformed tense client meetings by using what she calls the "60-second rule" - no interrupting for at least a minute, even if you disagree.

Solution-Oriented Approach: Don't dwell on problems - move toward solutions. Love how one of my tech leaders puts it: "Every complaint needs to come with at least one solution." A project manager turned "You're consistently missing deadlines" into "Let's understand what's blocking our timely delivery." The team opened up about resource constraints they'd been hesitant to mention.

The Power of "And": Instead of "You're creative but disorganized," try "You bring amazing creativity, and we need to find a way to organize these great ideas." Small shift, huge impact.

Pro Tip: Before any tough talk, "After this conversation, I want them to feel..." changes your whole approach.

Foster an environment that encourages continuous improvement. The art of delivering difficult messages lies in balancing honesty with humanity. Think of your words as bridges - they need to be both strong enough to carry the weight of truth and carefully constructed to maintain connection.

Diplomacy isn't about avoiding truth; it's about delivering it in a way that helps people hear it. So, stop trying to be diplomatic. Start trying to be helpful. The words will follow.

Recognizing the Storm: Identifying Difficult Conversations

The most challenging conversations often begin as subtle signals that, if missed, can escalate into larger issues. The earlier you spot these signs, the more options you have for addressing them constructively.

Performance Feedback

Watch for patterns of missed expectations or declining work quality. You'll notice team members avoiding regular check-ins, becoming defensive during reviews, or showing resistance to constructive input. A team member who previously welcomed feedback now responds to suggestions with "I know what I'm doing" or stops participating in team discussions.

Conflict Resolution

Look for signs of growing tension between team members - reduced collaboration, passive-aggressive comments, or competing rather than cooperating. Two department heads who once worked smoothly together now schedule separate meetings and communicate only through formal emails, signalling an underlying conflict needing attention.

Delivering Bad News

Recognize situations where significant changes will impact people's work or roles - budget cuts, project cancellations, or organizational shifts. When quarterly results show you'll need to pause a major initiative, the need for a difficult conversation becomes clear through the growing anxiety among team members who sense something's coming.

Addressing Sensitive Personal Issues

Notice changes in behaviour, attendance, or interaction patterns that suggest personal challenges affecting work. A usually punctual and engaged employee starts arriving late, appears distracted, and withdraws from team activities - signals that a supportive but difficult conversation may be needed.

Negotiating Disagreements

Identify when different perspectives or priorities create roadblocks to progress. Watch for repeated circular discussions, increasing frustration, or teams working in silos. Marketing insists on a quick launch while Engineering emphasizes more testing and the growing tension in planning meetings indicates a needed conversation about balancing speed and quality.

Preparing for Difficult Conversations

Let me share a simple but powerful way to prepare for those tough conversations that keep you up at night.

The PLAN Framework

- **Purpose**: Instead of "need to discuss low team morale," aim for "build a more engaged and supported team." Rather than "address budget overruns," focus on "ensure project sustainability while maintaining quality."
- **Listen**: Do your pre-work and replace vague concerns with specific observations. Not "sales are down" but "Q3 targets missed by 28% in three key accounts." Gather concrete examples and check multiple perspectives - what might that "difficult" client be experiencing that you haven't considered?
- **Anticipate**: Think through reactions and prepare accordingly. When restructuring teams, consider how both promoted and passed-over employees might respond. Plan for various scenarios - from quiet withdrawal to vocal resistance.
- **Navigate**: Prepare clear, constructive openings. Rather than "We need to talk about your performance," try "I'd like to understand what support you need to achieve your goals."

A regional manager told his team about an upcoming merger. Rather than simply announcing changes, he prepared by understanding each team member's career aspirations and concerns. His opening: "Let's explore how these changes align with your career growth goals."

Managing Emotions during Difficult Discussions

Let me share something that transformed how my clients learnt to handle emotionally charged moments. Think of emotions in tough conversations like weather - you can't control them, but you can definitely learn to navigate them.

Before walking into that difficult conversation, do what one of my most successful clients calls the "body scan." Racing heart?

Clenched jaw? They're not just physical symptoms - they're your emotional dashboard lighting up.

The Power Pause: When tension rises, use what a CEO calls her "oxygen mask" - "Give me a moment to think about that." Simple, yet it's saved countless crucial conversations from derailing.

The Perspective Flip: Instead of "Everything's falling apart," try "Here's what we can save." Had a client turn a crisis meeting around with just this shift.

Find your Centre in the Storm: Find your anchor - that simple practice or reminder that keeps you steady and let it guide you through the storm of difficult conversations. Maybe it's that deep breath before you speak, feeling your feet firmly on the ground, or remembering your core purpose.

An executive whom I know swears by the three-breath rule: three slow breaths before responding to anything that triggers strong emotions. These personal anchors aren't just coping mechanisms; they're your reset button, your reminder to respond rather than react

Pro Tip: Share your learnings with a trusted colleague - different perspectives reveal blind spots. Managing emotions isn't about suppressing them - it's about steering them toward solutions.

Crafting Your Message with Care

Words shape outcomes. In sensitive conversations, every phrase either builds bridges or burns them. Choose language that shows respect while staying true to your message.

Think of your message as a key - it needs to be precisely crafted to unlock understanding without breaking trust. Your tone isn't just about being nice, it's about being impactful.

The MESSAGE Model

- **M**indful: "How will these words land?" Consider saying "I see some areas where we could strengthen this" rather than "This isn't good enough"

- **E**mpathetic: Show you get it. "I understand this timeline is challenging" resonates better than "You're always behind schedule"
- **S**pecific: Use clear examples. Not "Your communication needs work" but "In yesterday's client meeting, when you..."
- **S**olution-focused: Move forward. "How can we prevent this in future?" instead of dwelling on "Why did this happen?"
- **A**ssertive: Be clear without being harsh. "This deadline is non-negotiable because..." rather than "You have to..."
- **G**entle: Your tone matters. "Let's explore why this happened" works better than "You need to explain this"
- **E**ncouraging: End with possibility. "I'm confident we can figure this out" rather than just listing problems

Every difficult conversation is an opportunity to strengthen, not strain, relationships.

The Language of Diplomacy

Refer to Table 7.1 for some power phrases that actually work in tough situations, tested in real business battlegrounds!

Table 7.1

When You Need To...	Instead of...	Try This...
Challenge Ideas	That won't work	I see your point about X. Have we considered Y?
Give Tough Feedback	Your performance is poor	I want to discuss some challenges I'm seeing, and explore solutions together
Express Disagreement	I disagree	Let me share a different perspective on this...
Handle Mistakes	You messed up	Let's understand what happened and how we can prevent it
Set Boundaries	That's impossible	Here's what we can realistically deliver...

When You Need To...	Instead of...	Try This...
Address Delays	You're late again	I notice our timelines are slipping. What support do you need?
Navigate Differences	That's not how we do it	Help me understand how this works in your context
Push Back	No, I can't take this up	Let me explain the challenges I see, and maybe we can find alternatives!
Express Urgency	Do it now	This is time-sensitive because... How can we make it happen?
Request Changes	This isn't good enough	To make this even better, we could...

The most effective messages aren't just heard - they're felt. They open doors to dialogue rather than shutting down discussion. Choose words that invite others into solution-finding rather than pushing them into defence.

Real-World Scenario: The Client Compromise

Imagine you're a project manager. Your biggest client wants to add features to a project without extending the deadline or budget. A diplomatic approach might look like this:

1. Acknowledge the client's desires: *I understand these new features are important to you.*
2. Express shared goals: *We're committed to delivering a product that exceeds your expectations.*
3. Present reality diplomatically: *To ensure the quality you are expecting, we'll need to discuss adjustments to our timeline or scope.*
4. Offer solutions: *Let's explore options that balance your new requests with our current constraints.*

Diplomacy is about finding the sweet spot between assertiveness and cooperation.

Managing Challenging Situations

When conversations become difficult, maintain focus on productive dialogue. If someone becomes defensive, acknowledge their perspective while gently redirecting to the core issues. For emotional responses, demonstrate empathy while maintaining professional boundaries.

Resistance often signals underlying concerns. Explore these through curious inquiry rather than confrontation. Look for common ground and shared objectives to move past initial resistance.

Check Table 7.2 for some actionable tips.

Table 7.2

When They Are	Do This	Avoid This
Defensive	I hear your concerns. Let's explore solutions together.	Stop being defensive
Disengaged	What are your thoughts on this? Your input matters	You need to pay attention
Emotional	Take the time you need. This is important	You're overreacting
Argumentative	Let's look at the facts together	You're wrong
Accepting	Great perspective. How can we build on this?	See, that wasn't so bad

Building Solutions Together

Great leaders turn battlegrounds into brainstorming sessions. For them, it's not about winning arguments but about winning together. Stop thinking "my solution vs. yours." Start pondering what could work for everyone?"

1. **Start Right**
   - Open with: "Let's put all ideas on the table first"
   - Focus on gathering, not judging

2. **Bridge Differences**
   - Use "Yes, and..." instead of "but"
   - Example: "Yes, the timeline is tight, and let's explore options"
3. **Find Common Ground**
   - Ask: "What does success look like for everyone?"
   - Collect ideas before discussing constraints

Afterall, the best solutions often live in the space between opposing views.

Learning from Difficult Conversations

Let me share some reflection questions for turning tough conversations into growth moments - straight from the trenches of leadership coaching.

1. What went well?
2. What could you have done differently?
3. What assumptions were you making?
4. What did you learn about yourself or the other person?
5. How can you apply this learning to future conversations?

Maybe some time later, you can even take a deeper dive.

Ask yourself: "What triggered you, and why?; Where did the energy shift?; What opened up the breakthrough?"

A Pharma CEO transformed his leadership style after noticing he always rushed to solutions instead of exploring emotions first.

Every difficult conversation is a masterclass if you're willing to learn from it.

Manage Professional Boundaries

Strong professional relationships require clear boundaries. Establish expectations about communication channels, response times, and escalation paths early in working relationships. Maintain these boundaries consistently while allowing appropriate flexibility for unique situations.

Documentation and Follow-Through

Document key discussion points, agreements, and next steps promptly after important conversations. Create a clear timeline for follow-up and monitoring progress. Regular check-ins help ensure accountability and provide opportunities to address challenges early.

Case Studies: Successful Navigation of Difficult Conversations

Each of the scenario below shows a common thread: success came not from perfect scripts but from genuine curiosity, a focus on shared goals, and the courage to move conversations beyond the immediate problem to deeper understanding.

The Client Relationship Rescue

A major client was threatening to end a five-year partnership over recent delivery delays. Rather than defending or apologizing, the account manager took an unexpected approach: "Before we discuss timelines, help me understand how these delays are impacting your business goals."

This shifted the conversation from blame to partnership. They discovered the client's real concern was looking unprepared to their board. Together, they created a new reporting structure that gave the client earlier visibility into potential delays.

The Remote Work Revolution

A traditional manufacturing company faced resistance when key team members requested hybrid work. Instead of a flat yes/no, the Operations Head opened with: "Help me understand what aspects of remote work would most impact your effectiveness."

The conversation revealed their top engineers needed focused time for complex calculations. The solution? Two remote days for deep work, three office days for collaboration. Productivity increased by 30%, and retention improved.

From Crisis to Innovation

When budget cuts forced a product team to reduce features, instead of simply announcing cuts, the product owner asked: "If we can only deliver three features that would delight our users, which would they be?"

This reframe turned a potential morale crisis into an innovation opportunity. The team actually improved the product by focusing on core value, and engagement increased despite reduced resources.

You can refer to Appendix D for more diplomatic communication scripts for workplace scenarios.

The Golden Rule: The most powerful tool in difficult conversations isn't what you say - it's how genuinely you seek to understand.

Chapter Wrap Up: Navigating Difficult Conversations

The true measure of success in difficult conversations isn't just reaching agreement or solving problems. It's in how people feel understood and valued through the process.

1. Your intention shapes the interaction. When you genuinely seek to understand rather than to prove a point, people feel it.
2. Silence is as powerful as words. Sometimes the best response is creating space for others to help them find their voice.
3. Every difficult conversation is an opportunity - to build trust, to deepen understanding, to strengthen relationships.

The next time you face a challenging conversation, remember: Your power lies not in having all the answers, but in being fully present with the questions.

In the end, it's not about mastering a technique - it's about bringing your full, authentic self to each interaction, prepared but not scripted, confident but not rigid, focused on understanding rather than winning. That's when difficult conversations become doorways to deeper connections and meaningful change.

CHAPTER 8

Forge Connections to Fuel Success: Networking for Business Growth

Ever walked into a business event and felt that mix of hope and nervousness? You know great connections are waiting to be made, but starting those conversations isn't always easy. Networking is simply the art of making connections in a professional context.

Think of it like joining a new group of friends who happen to work in your field. This chapter will show you how to transform those awkward "Hello, my name is..." moments into genuine connections that can open doors to exciting opportunities.

Understanding Modern Business Networking

In today's interconnected world, networking has evolved far beyond the traditional exchange of business cards. It's the invisible thread that weaves together successful careers, innovative partnerships, and thriving businesses. Whether through a LinkedIn connection or a coffee conversation, networking transforms possibilities into realities.

Think of business networking as your professional garden. Each connection you make is like planting a seed that could bloom into an opportunity, a future partnership, a career or a business breakthrough.

The secret to effective networking lies not in perfecting your elevator pitch, but in approaching each interaction with authentic curiosity. When you genuinely want to learn about their journeys, challenges, and aspirations, networking transforms from a dreaded task into an engaging exploration.

Approach each interaction with open-mindedness, showing genuine interest in others and a desire to learn something new.

Instead of thinking, "What can this person do for me?" ask yourself:

- What can I learn from this person?
- How might we help each other?
- What interesting stories might they have?

At your next event, challenge yourself to have meaningful conversations with at least three new people. Focus on learning something interesting about each person, not on what you can gain from them. Instead of: "I need to collect 20 business cards today." Try: "I'm going to learn three interesting industry insights and make two meaningful connections."

Setting Networking Goals

Define Clear Objectives

Vague goals like "meet new people" don't drive action. Instead, set specific targets:

- Connect with three potential clients in your industry
- Find two mentors in senior management positions
- Build relationships with five peers in similar roles

Choose Strategic Events

Research events where you'll meet your target connections like industry conferences, professional association meetings, skill-building workshops, local business meetups and online industry forums.

Do your pre-work

Before walking into that industry conference or virtual meetup, do your homework - know who's attending, understand their work, and prepare thoughtful questions that show genuine interest. When you meet someone, share relevant insights that add value to their challenges or celebrate their successes.

Creating a Lasting Impression: Perfecting Your First Impressions

First impressions are formed within seconds and can influence the entire course of a professional relationship. While appearance and handshakes matter, the true impact comes from deeper elements of connection.

The Psychology Behind First Meetings

Our brain makes rapid assessments of trustworthiness, competence, and likability within moments of meeting someone new. Understanding this psychology helps you present your best self authentically.

Mastering Communication Dynamics

Strong first impressions rely on the harmony between what you say and how you say it. Your voice should be clear and measured, while your body language remains open and receptive. Simple gestures like maintaining eye contact and nodding thoughtfully demonstrate genuine interest.

The Power of Authentic Connection

Authentic charm wins over practiced perfection. Rather than rehearsing scripts or putting on a persona, show genuine interest in others. Share relevant experiences that highlight your values and expertise naturally.

Initiating Conversations: Mastering the Art of Small Talk

Begin with a simple "Hello" and your name. A genuine smile and relaxed posture make others comfortable. Everyone at networking events is there to connect, so your initiative is usually welcome.

Start with shared experiences: the venue, an interesting speaker, or recent industry news. Questions like "What brings you to this event?" create natural openings for deeper discussion. Focus on finding common ground rather than impressing.

The FORM Technique

Guide conversations naturally through these topics:

- **Family:** Discuss hometown or local connections
- **Occupation:** Explore professional role and responsibilities
- **Recreation:** Share recent exciting experiences/interests or hobbies
- **Motivation:** Discuss industry passions/driving factors

Situational Awareness

Let your environment inspire conversation. At conferences, discuss upcoming sessions. In co-working spaces, talk about projects. These contextual topics feel natural and relevant, making connections easier and more authentic.

The Pitch Perfector: Crafting Your Elevator Pitch

Communicating Your Value Proposition

The Core Elements

Start with a clear, engaging introduction that goes beyond your job title. Instead of "I'm a project manager," say "I help teams deliver complex projects that drive business growth." Focus on the value you bring and the problems you solve.

Tailoring Your Message

Adapt your introduction based on your audience. When speaking with a marketing executive, emphasize your brand-building achievements. With a tech leader, highlight your digital transformation successes. Keep it relevant to their interests and potential collaboration opportunities.

Sharing Success Stories

Include one brief, specific achievement. "My team's recent digital campaign increased client engagement by 50% in three months" is more memorable than general statements. Make your impact tangible and measurable.

The SPAR Framework

- Situation: Your current role and context
- Passion: What drives your work
- Achievement: A specific, impressive result
- Request: A clear next step or connection point

Example: "I run digital campaigns at MarketPro, specializing in B2B tech. I get excited about turning complex products into compelling stories. Recently, our video series helped a client triple their qualified leads. What's your experience been with B2B content marketing?"

Keep your entire introduction under 30 seconds, natural in tone, and focused on opening a conversation rather than closing a sale.

Building Meaningful Connections: REAL Approach

Remember four key elements in every interaction:

- Relate through common ground
- Engage with genuine interest
- Add value where you can
- Link people to opportunities

Real relationships matter more than rehearsed pitches. Think of the REAL approach not as a formula but as a mindset for authentic engagement. Start by finding common ground - maybe you both struggle with remote team dynamics or share a passion for mentoring.

Show real curiosity about others' journeys; ask questions that make people think, not just talk. When you share with a tech lead insight about a challenge he is going through, you're building trust through tangible value.

When someone mentions their project challenges, respond with specifics like *"I faced similar data privacy issues in my healthcare app. Would you like to hear how we solved it?"* This transforms casual conversation into valuable exchange.

Or: *"You mentioned needing UX designers. I know an excellent one from my last project. Shall I make an introduction?"*

Another example: *"I saw your company's expanding to Singapore. When I opened our Asia office, local networking groups were crucial. I can introduce you to some key contacts there if you'd like."*

One meaningful connection can open more doors than dozens of superficial ones. Like that CTO who landed my client her dream role not through applying, but through a coffee chat that revealed aligned visions about technology's future.

The Golden Rule: Every strong professional relationship start with someone offering genuine help or sharing relevant experience. Focus on what you can give, not what you can get.

Networking Etiquettes and Best Practices

Good networking etiquette isn't about rigid rules, it's about making others feel valued and respected in every interaction.

Professional Conduct That Works

"Thanks for sharing your insights about renewable energy, Raha. I have some research about solar trends that might interest you. May I send it over?" This approach demonstrates value before asking for anything in return.

Cultural Awareness in Action

When networking internationally, adjust your style. In Japan, exchange business cards with both hands and take time to read them.

In the Middle East, build personal rapport before discussing business. Simple awareness of these customs shows respect and builds trust.

Give and Take Balance

Instead of asking "Can you introduce me to your marketing team?" try "*I noticed you're expanding your social media presence. Our team just completed a similar project. Would sharing our learnings help?*"

Follow-Up that Works

Reach out within 24 hours of meeting someone new. This shows enthusiasm and helps cement the connection while it's still fresh.

Instead of the generic "Let's keep in touch," try: "*I'm testing a solution similar to what you mentioned. I'll share our findings next week. Would that be helpful?*"

Follow-Up Email Templates for Networking Success

Basic Connection Follow-Up

Hi Aysha,

Great meeting you at yesterday's Digital Summit. Your insights about blockchain in finance were fascinating.

I found this recent case study on DeFi adoption that aligns with your project. Would you find it helpful if I shared it?

Would love to continue our discussion. Free for a 15-minute coffee chat next week?

Regards,

Ashish

Value-Adding Follow-Up

Hi Shashi,

I really enjoyed our conversation about startup scaling at the Founders Meetup.

You mentioned struggling with developer recruitment. I've worked with an excellent tech talent agency that might help. Would you like an introduction?

Regards,

Ruchi

Conference Connection Follow-Up

Hi David,

Your presentation on data privacy at TechCon was eye-opening. Especially interested in your points about GDPR compliance.

Since you're expanding to Europe, thought you might find our recent compliance toolkit useful. Happy to share it if helpful.

Available for a brief call to explore potential collaboration? Regards,

Lisa

Key elements in each email:

- Reference where you met
- Mention specific conversation points
- Offer concrete value
- Suggest clear next steps

Networking in the Digital Age

The digital world hasn't changed the heart of networking - it's still about authentic connection and mutual value. However, it demands more intentional effort to create warmth through screens while offering unprecedented opportunities to maintain meaningful connections across borders and time zones.

Building Your Digital Presence

Your LinkedIn profile is your virtual first impression. Include a professional photo, compelling headline, and brief achievements. Example headline: "Driving Digital Innovation | AI Solutions Architect | Speaker on Tech Ethics"

Engaging Effectively Online

Instead of "Great post!", comment with value: *"Your points about AI ethics remind me of my recent project implementing facial recognition. One challenge we faced was... What's your take on handling bias in these systems?"* Also, one thoughtful comment beats ten generic likes.

Strategic Platform Use

LinkedIn: Share industry insights and project updates *"Just wrapped up an AI implementation that cut customer response time by 60%. Happy to share learnings - drop a comment if interested."*

Virtual Event Networking

Don't just attend virtual events - arrive 10 minutes early to spark casual conversations in the chat and stay 5 minutes after to exchange contact details with speakers and fellow attendees who resonated with you.

The real power comes from mastering the digital small talk - drop relevant emojis, share quick insights in the chat, and use the platform's networking features like breakout rooms to create memorable micro- connections that can blossom into valuable professional relationships.

Chapter Wrap Up: Your Networking Action Plan

Daily Practices

Start small: Reach out to one connection daily. *"Hi Teresa, your recent project launch looked impressive. Would love to hear what worked best."*

Conversation Starters That Work

Keep these ready:

- What's the most exciting project you're working on?
- How did you navigate your industry shift? I'm considering a similar move.
- "What emerging trend in our field interests you most?

Active Listening in Action
During conversations, look for opportunities to dig deeper:

- "That's fascinating - how did you handle the technical challenges?
- What made you choose that particular approach?

Your Professional Story
Test this format: "I help [target audience] achieve [specific outcome] through [your unique approach]. Recently, I [specific achievement]."

Follow-Up Strategy
Within 24 hours: Send a personalized note within a week: Share a relevant resource within a month: Suggest a catch-up call

Afterall, effective networking isn't about perfection, it's about consistent, authentic connection.

CHAPTER 9

Executive Communication: Inspire and Influence to Maximize Impact

Leadership speaks louder than words, but words give leadership its voice. In the C-suite, every word carries weight. When executives speak, markets move, careers pivot, and teams mobilize. Great communication turns strategy into story, vision into victory.

In this chapter, we'll decode the communication strategies of exceptional leaders, showing you how to transform everyday messages into moments that matter. We'll unlock the communication approaches that can enable executives to transform complex ideas into compelling narratives, navigate crucial conversations, and inspire lasting change.

Verbal Tattoos that Leave a Lasting Mark

What if executive one-liners are the new power suits! A powerful one-liner can be the difference between being remembered and being forgotten.

Cement your Executive Brand with your impactful one-liner, here are a few to inspire you.

- Our success is measured by the success of those we serve.
- Our competition sells services. We deliver transformation.
- Our team doesn't have employees. We have game-changers.

- Disruption isn't just a buzzword here. It's our business model.
- We don't follow best practices. We define them.
- We're not building a company. We're shaping an industry.
- We don't just raise the bar. We redefine what the bar means.
- Our Return on Investment isn't just financial. It's societal.
- We don't follow or predict trends. We set them.
- We turn setbacks into comebacks.
- In our company, innovation isn't a department. It's everyone's job.
- We're not just disrupting markets. We're creating new ones.
- In our playbook, 'good enough' is the enemy of greatness.
- In a world of followers, we cultivate leaders.
- We don't just adapt to change. We are the change.
- In a world of instant gratification, we're playing the long game.
- We don't just solve problems. We prevent them.
- Others see data. We see stories waiting to be told.
- Our strategy isn't to be the best in the world but to be the best for the world!

Real Leadership: Where Authenticity Meets Vulnerability

The most powerful leadership tool isn't authority, it is authenticity. In a world obsessed with projecting perfection, real leadership takes a different path. It's about having the courage to be genuine, the wisdom to share failures, and the strength to show vulnerability.

Transform Experience into Leadership Wisdom

Every experience you've had, shapes how you lead today.

"I started as a programmer in my garage. Back then, I learned that creating something new isn't about fancy technology, it's about fixing real problems people have. That's why our company now focuses on solutions that actually help our customers, not just the latest trends."

Convert Setbacks into Comebacks

Your tough times can help you redefine your strategy.

"Early in my sales career, I learned that every 'no' isn't a rejection. It's a roadmap to your next 'yes.' This insight drives our current strategy: we're systematically connecting with every customer who left us last year, not to win them back, but to build something worth coming back to."

Embrace Vulnerability as a Catalyst

Acknowledging challenges doesn't diminish leadership, it amplifies its impact.

"Last month our team worked three nights straight to meet a deadline. That's not something to celebrate, it's a sign we need to change. Here's my plan to make sure it never happens again..."

Turn Mistakes into Movement

When leaders openly acknowledge missteps, they create a culture of continuous learning.

"I'll be direct: our Asian market expansion moved too aggressively and strained our teams to breaking point. Here's what this taught us about sustainable growth, and here's our refined approach to building a lasting global presence."

Leading With Your Values

Your core values should be your leadership compass.

"Missing my child's graduation ceremony taught me what matters most. From now on, no meetings after 6 PM. Good leadership isn't about giving up your personal life, it's about finding a better way to integrate work and life together."

Beyond Buzzwords: The Art of Meaningful Communication

Great communication isn't about using fancy words or technical jargon. It's about making your message resonate with real people in real situations.

Making Complex Ideas Simple

The best leaders help people see what changes mean for them. When Alan Jope outlined Unilever's sustainability push, he skipped the environmental jargon. Instead, he said: *"Every product we sell must do good for both people and planet."*

A complex business overhaul became a clear daily mission for thousands.

Consider these two announcements:

1. We're implementing a digital transformation initiative to optimize operational efficiency.
2. We're bringing in new tools that will cut your paperwork in half and let you spend more time with clients.

The second version shows executive communication at its best, turning business strategy into clear personal impact.

Connecting Vision to Action

Strong executive communication links the big picture to daily work:

"We're not just chasing 30% growth; we're helping small businesses thrive. When you show a shop owner how to use our platform, you're giving them back precious time with their family."

Real Leaders, Real Talk

Some leaders get this just right:

Microsoft (Satya Nadella)

Instead of diving into technical specs, he said: *"Think of cloud computing like electricity - it's going to change how everyone works, learns, and creates."*

Apple (Tim Cook)

Rather than talking about data protocols, he put it simply: *"Your information is yours, period. That's not just our policy - it's our belief."*

Transform Corporate-speak into Human speech

- Not "optimize synergies" but "help teams work better together"
- Not "leverage assets" but "make the most of what we have"
- Not "implement cost reduction" but "spend wisely to protect jobs"

The best messages don't sound like they came from a boardroom. They sound like one person talking to another about something that matters to both of them.

The Golden Rule: If you wouldn't say it over coffee, don't say it in a company memo.

Stakeholder Engagement: Building Trust

Success in modern business hinges on the ability to build and maintain strong relationships with multiple stakeholder groups with their unique expectations, concerns, and communication preferences. Map out various stakeholder groups -investors, board members, employees, customers, regulators, community.

From board members seeking strategic insight to employees needing operational clarity, from customers demanding transparency to regulators requiring compliance documentation - each group requires a distinct communication approach.

The Art of Adaptive Communication

The three-dimensional approach to communication is the art of flexibly adjusting your message and delivery style based on your audience's preferences and needs (**people**), the specific context or purpose of the interaction (**situation**), and the physical or cultural setting where the communication takes place (**environment**).

Consider how Amazon's same-day delivery meant different things to different people:

- **To customers:** "*Get what you need, when you need it today.*"

- **To investors:** "*We're doubling our market reach and increasing purchase frequency.*"
- **To employees:** "*You're helping busy families spend more time together.*"

Or take Satya Nadella discussing Microsoft's AI integration:

- **To developers:** "*GPT-4 APIs now integrate directly with your existing Azure workflows.*"
- **To enterprise clients:** "*Your teams will create presentations in minutes instead of hours.*"
- **To shareholders:** "*We're turning AI from a lab experiment into daily business value.*"

Shifting with Situations

High-Stakes Situations

- During crisis: "*Here's what happened, here's what we're doing, here's when it'll be fixed.*"
- Strategic planning: "*Market shifts have opened three specific opportunities...*"

Growth Conversations

- **Team sessions:** *Each of you is writing our next chapter of success.*
- **Innovation talks:** *Let's reimagine what's possible for our customers.*

Adapting to Environment

Formal Settings

- **In the boardroom:** *Our Q3 results show 15% growth, driven by three strategic initiatives...*
- **At client meetings:** *Our partnership has cut processing time by 30%...*

Informal Moments

- **Over coffee:** *Let me share what we're seeing from customers using our new feature...*
- **During a walk:** *As we head to lunch, I'll outline where the team's heading next...*

The most effective communicators read three dimensions – who they're talking to, where they are, and what the moment demands. When these align, information doesn't just flow; it resonates and drives action.

Providing Constructive Feedback

I often tell my clients - feedback is like an alternative medicine. The right dose at the right time heals; the wrong approach can make things worse.

Think of feedback like a bridge, it connects where someone is to where they could be. The best feedback conversations don't tear down, they build up. They're not lectures, they're growth partnerships. They are like regular "coffee catchups" where feedback flows naturally both ways.

Here's a truth bomb: sandwiching negative feedback between compliments? Your team sees through that faster than free pizza disappears from the break room. Instead, try what I call the "growth conversation" approach. Start with "*I'm sharing this because I see your potential*" - this changes everything.

A mentor made me learn this lesson early in my career, "*People don't remember what you said; they remember how you made them feel.*"

Setting the Stage: Before diving in

You must align yourself before you start giving critical feedback.

- Ask yourself: What do I want for this person?
- Choose the right moment and private space
- Prepare specific examples, not general observations

Opening the Dialogue

The first moments set the tone. Choose your opener based on the situation:

- **For regular check-ins:** *I'd love to reflect together on how things are going. Before I share my thoughts, how do you feel things have been going with [project/area]?*
- **When improvement is needed:** *I'm having this conversation because I see your potential and want to help you succeed. I've noticed some areas where we could work together to help you have even more impact. Would you be open to exploring those?*
- **For specific behaviours:** *I wanted to talk about what I observed in [situation]. Before I share my thoughts, what was your experience of that moment?*
- **For career development:** *I see several opportunities for your growth. First, I'd love to hear about your career aspirations and where you'd like to develop.*

The Growth Conversation Framework

1. **Start with Possibility:** *I'm sharing this because I see your ability to lead major projects.*
2. **Share What You See:** *During Tuesday's meeting, I noticed you seemed hesitant to speak up.*
3. **Discuss Real Impact:** *This meant we missed your valuable insights on the customer data.*
4. **Explore solutions:** *What are your thoughts on approaching this differently?*

When things get difficult

- **Stay curious:** *Help me understand what's happening.*
- **Acknowledge feelings:** *I hear this is frustrating.*
- **Focus on partnership:** *Let's figure this out together.*

End with crystal clarity

- What we discussed
- Specific actions to take

- When to check in next
- Support needed

Power Phrases That Work

- *I'm curious about your perspective...*
- *What I've noticed is...*
- *How can I help you succeed?*
- *Let's be specific about next steps...*

The best feedback isn't about pointing out what's wrong, it's about illuminating what's possible. Build the relationship first, and even tough messages land on a fertile ground.

Managing Meetings That Actually Matter

The best meetings aren't about covering an agenda - they're about uncovering solutions. Or as one wise CTO puts it: "If people leave your meeting without clarity on the next steps, you've just hosted a coffee break." Because meetings are expensive - not just in time, but in energy and opportunity cost. Make them count.

An executive abides by this rule in her team meetings: "If we're meeting, we're deciding." Everything else? That's an email or Slack thread. Suddenly, meetings became moments of action, not information dumps.

Every effective meeting answer three questions before it starts:

- Why are we meeting?
- Why these people?
- Why now?

State your destination: *"By the end of our time together, we need to [specific outcome]. We have [X] minutes to get there."*
Start strong: *"We have 30 minutes to decide our Q4 marketing strategy. By the end of this meeting, we need specific campaigns and owners for each initiative."*

Meeting Types and Scripts

Performance Reviews

Opening: "*Let's look at our metrics against targets.*"

For Challenges:

- What's causing this gap?
- What's our plan to correct course?
- What support do you need?

For Wins:

- What worked here?
- How do we repeat this success?
- Should we aim higher?

Project Updates

Begin with: Green means on track, yellow needs attention, red is blocked. We'll focus on yellow and red items only.

For Each Issue:

- What's the blocker?
- What solutions have we tried?
- What do we need to move forward?

Keeping Control

- Getting Back on Track: *"We have 15 minutes left and still need to decide pricing. Let's focus there."*
- Managing Tangents: *"That's valuable for another discussion. Let's note it and return to today's goal."*
- Engaging Everyone: *"Sarah, with your sales experience, what do you see here?"*

Closing Strong

End every meeting with:

1. Clear decisions made
2. Specific owners for each action

3. Firm deadlines
4. Next check-in date

Power Phrases for Meetings

- *"Let's start with our desired outcome..."*
- *"To respect everyone's time..."*
- *"Let's get specific about who does what..."*
- *"Our next step is..."*
- *"To summarize our decisions/actions..."*

The best meetings aren't about covering an agenda - they're about uncovering solutions. Keep meetings focused, action-oriented, and worth everyone's time.

Making Data Human: From Numbers to Narratives

In leadership, it's not just what the numbers say, it's how you make them speak. Numbers tell facts, but stories drive decisions. The art lies in making numbers relatable, turning metrics into meaning. The magic happens when you turn raw data into compelling stories that drive real understanding and action.

Here's how to make every number tell its story by refering to Table 9.1:

Table 9.1

Technique	Plain Data	Narrative Impact
Humanize Numbers	Customer base grew by 2M	*We welcomed enough new customers to fill 20 football stadiums*
	23% churn in Q3	*We're losing 1 in 4 customers - mostly in their first month*
	$1.2M revenue impact	*Each team member added $4K monthly to our bottom line*
	Saved 1,000 work hours	*Everyone got back a full week to focus on what matters most.*

Technique	Plain Data	Narrative Impact
	Generated $500K savings	*We saved enough to fund three new innovation projects.*
Relatable Comparisons	Customer acquisition cost is $342	*We spend a coffee a day for a customer who stays 3 years*
	Processing time reduced 66%	*What took an hour now takes 20 minutes*
	35% market penetration	*1 in 3 businesses in our city trusts us*
	Process is 70% faster	*What used to take a full workday now happens before lunch*
	Reduced carbon by 50,000 tons	*Like taking 10,000 cars off the road for a year*
Memorable Metaphors	Market volatility increased	*The market's behaving like a roller coaster - we need seatbelts fastened*
	Mobile engagement up 45%	*Users now spend their lunch break with us instead of just a coffee break*
	48% feature adoption	*Half our users haven't discovered our best tools yet*
	Complex project coordination	*We're conducting an orchestra of 50 different instruments - every note matters*
	Rapid company growth	*We're not just climbing the corporate ladder, we're building an elevator*

Data should illuminate, not intimidate. Make it clear, make it relevant, make it actionable because people don't want data, they want clarity.

From Uncertainty to Understanding: How to Talk About Change?

Change isn't just about new processes - it's about people. The most brilliant strategies fail when leaders can't bring their teams along the journey. The best leaders don't just announce change; they invite people into a compelling story about tomorrow.

Building the Change Narrative

- **Connect Past to Future:** "*We're building on our 20 years of customer trust to solve tomorrow's challenges.*"
- **Make It Personal:** "*This change gives each of you new opportunities to grow and make bigger impact* "
- **Announcing Change:** "*Our industry is changing. We can either shape that change or be shaped by it.*"
- **Technology Upgrade:** "*We're giving you tools that will cut your admin time in half.*"
- **Market Shift:** "*Our customers' needs are evolving. Here's how we'll grow with them.*"

Addressing Concerns

- **Acknowledge**: "*I know this brings up questions about your role and future.*"
- **Commit**: "*My priority is ensuring you have clarity and support through this transition.*"

Consider how different leaders navigate major transitions:

Adobe's Masterclass

Traditional approach: *"We're ending perpetual licenses for subscription models."*
Vision-led approach: *"Imagine having the latest creative tools at your fingertips, always updated, always ready. From students to studios, everyone gets to create without limits. That's the future we're building together."*

IBM's Leadership Lesson

Traditional approach: *"Restructuring for technological advancement."*
Purpose-driven approach: *"Each generation of IBMers has carried our legacy forward. Now it's our turn to reinvent IBM for our era. This is our moment to shape tomorrow."*

Essential Elements

1. Clear Vision
    - Where we're going
    - Why it matters
    - What success looks like
2. Personal Impact
    - What changes
    - What stays the same
    - How to succeed
3. Next Steps
    - Immediate actions
    - Available support
    - Timeline milestones

Great change communication doesn't sell the change, it sells the destination. It doesn't push people forward; it pulls them toward something better.

The Golden Rule: People don't resist change, they resist uncertainty. Your job isn't to eliminate all questions but to make the journey feel worth taking.

Crisis Communication: When Every Word Matters

Every crisis is a leadership moment. When things go wrong, all eyes turn to the top - not just for information, but for confidence that someone is in command. How you communicate in these moments can either accelerate the crisis or accelerate the recovery.

Speed matters, but accuracy matters more. Early in a crisis, it's okay to say, "We're investigating the full scope of the issue" rather than sharing unconfirmed details. Your first message sets the tone for trust.

The Three-Part Crisis Formula:

1. Situation: Clear facts about what happened
2. Action: Specific steps being taken
3. Next Steps: What to expect and what to do

Real Leaders in Real Crises

Microsoft's Service Crisis: *"Teams is down in Europe. Engineers are rerouting traffic to backup servers. Expect restoration in 2 hours, with updates every 15 minutes on our status page."*

Marriott's Security Response: *"Unauthorized database access detected. Systems secured, FBI cyber team engaged. Free credit monitoring available for all guests - enrolment link below."*

Tailoring Your Message

For Clients:

- What's happening
- Timeline for fix
- What they should do now

For Teams:

- Technical specifics
- Required actions
- Update schedule

For Leadership:

- Business impact
- Resource needs
- Strategic implications

Crisis Leadership: The Dimon's Approach

To the Board, he brought clarity: *"Three specific market risks identified. Our defense strategy and opportunity plans are ready."*

To Investors, he showed courage: *"We're choosing long-term stability over short-term profits. Here's why that matters."*

To Employees, he offered certainty: *"You've heard the headlines. Here's what it means for you: Your jobs are secure. Keep serving clients."*

To Partners, he built confidence: *"We're strong enough to support your growth. Here's concrete proof of our commitment."*

Core Principles

- Share what you know
- Acknowledge what you don't
- Focus on next steps
- Stay accessible
- Keep updates regular

The Golden Rule: In crisis, people need a leader more than a speaker. Give them confidence through clarity, care through action, and hope through honest progress.

Championing Diversity and Inclusion

Great inclusion isn't a special effort, it's built into how we work, talk, and decide. It's about making every voice count, naturally and consistently.

By saying, "*Who hasn't had a chance to weigh in yet?*", you make space for every voice.

A senior leader whom I know starts critical meetings with: *"We need three perspectives before we move forward - and they can't all come from the same department, level, or background."*

Everyday inclusive language is outlined in the Table 9.2

Table 9.2

Replace	With
Hey guys	Team, Everyone, Folks
Manpower	Workforce, Staff, Team
He/his (default)	They/their or specific pronouns
Master/slave (tech)	Primary/secondary, Leader/follower

Handling Tough Moments:

- When someone's interrupted: *"Let's circle back - Marya, you were sharing something important..."*
- When credit is misattributed: *"Yes, and that builds on Aisha's original insight about..."*

- When assumptions surface: "*That's interesting, how might different customer groups see this?*"

Power Phrases

- *Who hasn't shared their perspective yet?*
- *Let's hear from someone with a different experience.*
- *What other angles should we consider?*

True inclusion is about creating space where everyone feels valued and heard.

Elevating Communication with Idioms

- *"With the new product launch approaching, I've got a lot on my plate. Our supply chain is facing delays, and we still need board approval, there's no room for error."*
- *"When discussing our expansion plans, we can't put all our eggs in one basket. We should consider parallel entry into emerging Asian markets."*
- *"While tech giants have deep pockets, we can leverage our startup's agility to carve out our niche."*
- *"Our hands are tied when it comes to hiring more developers this quarter."*
- *"The merger negotiations have hit a deadlock over valuation. We need to hold all the aces before our next meeting. Having concrete data about our market potential will strengthen our position."*
- *"In tomorrow's investor meeting, we'll need to keep our cards close to our chest about the upcoming acquisition."*
- *"Let's lay all our cards on the table about our Q3 performance. While we missed our revenue targets, I see light at the end of the tunnel. Our new product line is showing promising early results."*
- *"Our business meetings are opportunities to build trust through clear, strategic communication. Every word should serve your message, not overshadow it."*

Executive Communication Playbook: From Information to Impact

From my years of helping leaders transform their conversations, I've developed a playbook of proven approaches that turn standard corporate messages into communications that drive real impact. Think of it as your guide to making every word count.

Check out Table 9.3 for some detailed examples of power messaging for various business situations.

Table 9.3

Leadership Moment	Traditional Message	Power Message
Lead with Purpose	We're investing $50M in automation technology.	To give our customers faster service and our teams less paperwork, we're bringing in new tools.
Simplify Complexity	We're leveraging distributed ledger technology to optimize transactions.	We're making payments as easy as sending a text message.
Bridge Past & Future	Our Q4 metrics necessitate a strategic pivot.	The same courage that made us pioneers in home delivery will now make us leaders in sustainable packaging.
Tell Stories, Not Stats	Our NPS increased by 15 points.	Remember Sonia? She just told us we've become her easiest vendor to work with.
Navigate Tough News	Market conditions have necessitated a workforce optimization.	We're facing the toughest market in our history. Here's why, here's how we'll help, here's our path forward.
Focus on Outcomes	We're implementing a multi-channel engagement strategy.	By next quarter, customers will get help in three clicks instead of three calls.
Create Connection	This merger creates significant market synergies.	By joining forces with ABC Corp, you'll have twice the opportunities for growth.

Chapter Wrap Up: Your Executive Communication Toolkit

Great executive communication isn't about being polished – it's about being clear, authentic, and purposeful in every interaction.

Core Communication Pillars

1. **Clarity Over Complexity**
   - Transform complex strategies into clear, actionable messages
   - Focus on "what this means for us" in every message
2. **Authentic Leadership**
   - Share both successes and learning moments
   - Lead with vulnerability and transparent communication
3. **Stakeholder-Centric Approach**
   - Connect organizational goals to stakeholder benefits
   - Tailor messages for different audience needs
   - Managing crisis communication with poise
4. **Story-Driven Communication**
   - Present data within human context
   - Use real examples to illustrate impact
   - Create memorable narratives that inspire action

   The most powerful executive communication happens when you:
   - Prioritize clarity over corporate speak
   - Share authentic experiences over polished presentations
   - Focus on human impact over raw metrics
   - Create dialogue over one-way broadcasts

The real power comes from making Executive communication a bridge from vision to action. Let every word drive impact, every message build trust, and every interaction move your team forward.

CHAPTER 10

Tailored Communication: Strategies and Scripts for Business Functions

Effective communication is not a one-size-fits-all approach; each department within an organization has its own unique challenges, objectives, and audience. The leaders and managers must navigate a complex web of stakeholder expectations, team dynamics, and business objectives.

This chapter provides a structured approach to departmental communications, offering practical scripts and strategies scripts designed to meet the specific needs of various departments.

Communication Dimensions in Practice

Understanding when to use which communication style and framework can significantly impact leadership effectiveness and organizational success.

We can understand the multi-dimensional nature of organizational communication through two essential frameworks - one organized by communication context (internal, external, and crisis communications) and another by communication purpose (strategic, operational, and event-based interactions).

Understanding Communication Context

Communication in organizations flows across three critical dimensions: internal, external, and crisis communications. Each dimension requires distinct approaches, tones, and strategies to ensure message effectiveness.

The Table 10.1 breaks down these contexts into actionable components, helping leaders navigate various communication scenarios they encounter in their roles.

Table 10.1:

Internal Communication	External Communication	Crisis Communication
• Team Meetings • Cross-functional Communication • Performance Reviews • Reviews Strategic	• Clients Engagement • Vendor/Partner Interactions • Public Relations • Media Interactions	• Emergency Response • Issue Management • Recovery Communication • Prevention Strategy

Understanding Communication Purpose

Every business communication serves a specific purpose, whether it's driving strategic initiatives, managing daily operations, or responding to specific events and contexts.

Understanding these three fundamental types - strategic, operational, and event-based communication enables leaders to align their messaging with organizational objectives and timelines while ensuring appropriate impact at every level.

Table 10.2 gives detailed examples of each type of communication.

Table 10.2:

Aspect	Strategic Communication	Operational Communication	Event-based Communication
Purpose	• Sets organizational direction • Drives major transformation • Establishes long-term goals	• Ensures smooth daily operations • Maintains performance standards • Facilitates routine coordination	• Addresses specific situations • Manages change initiatives • Responds to opportunities/ challenges

Aspect	Strategic Communication	Operational Communication	Event-based Communication
Examples	• Vision and Mission • Market Positioning • Goals Alignment • Change Management • Risk Assessment and Mitigation • Annual Updates	• Project Management • Quality Control • Client Delivery • Performance Tracking • Daily Huddles • Monthly/Quarterly Reviews • Project Updates • Resource Management	• Training Programs • Project Launches • Crisis Response • Special Announcements • Growth Discussions • Innovation Planning

The following sections in this chapter will help leaders identify and execute the right communication approach based on the purpose, stakeholders and impact level of different business scenarios.

HR Department Scripts

1. Team Review Meeting

"As we reflect on this month's achievements and challenges, let's assess how our HR strategies are strengthening our workforce and culture.

Agenda:

1. Recruitment metrics review
   - Open positions status
   - Time-to-fill metrics
   - Quality of hire indicators
   - Recruitment pipeline health
2. Employee relations update
   - Ongoing cases
   - Resolution status
   - Preventive measures
3. Training program status
4. Policy implementation updates
5. Team workload distribution

Let's examine our people metrics and refine our approach to drive organizational excellence…"

2. New Employee Onboarding Session

"Welcome to an organization where every individual's contribution matters. Today marks the beginning of your journey with us – one that we hope will be rewarding and impactful. We're excited to immerse you in our culture and set you up for success in your role…

Agenda:

1. Company overview
    - Mission, vision, and values
    - Organization structure
    - Key stakeholders
2. HR policies and procedures
3. Benefits explanation
    - Healthcare coverage
    - Leave policies
    - Insurance details
4. IT systems and access
5. Q&A session

Let's begin with our company's journey..."

3. Recruitment Planning Meeting with Department Heads

"Thank you for joining this recruitment planning session. Our goal is to align hiring needs with departmental objectives. Let's design recruitment approaches that attract exceptional talent to fuel our success…

Agenda:

1. Current workforce analysis
2. Upcoming project requirements

3. Skills gap assessment
4. Timeline planning
    - Job description finalization
    - Interview panel formation
    - Assessment criteria
5. Budget considerations

Let's start by reviewing your department's growth projections..."

4. Training Program Launch

"We're launching an initiative that will elevate our organizational capabilities and individual growth. Let's kick off a program that will enhance our collective potential and strengthen our competitive edge...

Agenda:

1. Skill development priorities
    - Technical skills
    - Soft skills
    - Leadership development
2. Training schedule
3. Assessment methods
4. Success metrics
5. Resource allocation

The program has been designed based on our recent skills assessment..."

5. Performance Review Calibration

"Fair performance assessment demands alignment. Today we'll calibrate our performance standards to ensure consistent and fair evaluations. Let's align on performance metrics that recognize and reward excellence effectively...

Agenda:

1. Review framework
   - Rating definitions
   - Assessment parameters
   - Documentation requirements
2. Common biases awareness
3. Case study discussions
4. Moderation process
5. Timeline and deadlines

Let's begin by reviewing our performance matrix..."

6. Employee Relations Issues

"Creating positive employee experiences requires addressing challenges proactively. Today we'll focus on strengthening our employee relations framework. Let's tackle these workplace dynamics with empathy and strategic thinking…

Agenda:

1. Issue overview
   - Nature of concerns
   - Affected departments
   - Impact assessment
2. Investigation findings
3. Proposed solutions
4. Communication strategy
5. Preventive measures

Let's start with the most common concern that we have found out..."

7. Compensation Review Meeting

"Competitive compensation drives retention, Today we'll evaluate our reward frameworks to maintain our position as an employer of choice.

Let's align our compensation strategies with both market trends and organizational values…

Agenda:

1. Market analysis
   - Industry benchmarks
   - Competitor offerings
   - Cost of living adjustments
2. Budget considerations
3. Performance linkage
4. Implementation strategy
5. Communication plan

Let's begin with industry trends..."

8. HR Crisis Management: Workplace Incident

"We're here to address a sensitive workplace matter with both urgency and care. This workplace situation demands immediate, thoughtful action to protect our people and values. Let's focus on resolving this situation while maintaining trust and organizational stability…

Agenda:

1. Incident details
   - Nature of incident
   - Parties involved
   - Immediate actions taken
2. Legal compliance check
3. Investigation process
4. Communication strategy
5. Preventive measures

Let's start with the incident report..."

Sales Team Scripts

1. Monthly Sales Team Review

"As we enter our next growth phase, it's critical we develop robust strategies to expand our footprint within our key accounts. Today we'll decode our sales metrics to sharpen our competitive edge and market penetration. Let's examine how our strategies are converting to successful client partnerships and revenue growth...

Agenda:

1. Pipeline review
   - New opportunities
   - Closing probability
   - Risk assessment
2. Win/Loss analysis
3. Customer feedback
4. Resource requirements
5. Next week's priorities

Starting with our top opportunities..."

2. Client Quarterly Business Review

"Our partnership has created significant value, let's explore how we can amplify this success. Today we'll evaluate our shared journey and chart an even more ambitious path forward. Let's examine how our collaboration is driving mutual growth and identify new opportunities...

Agenda:

1. Performance review
   - Service delivery metrics
   - SLA adherence
   - Issue resolution status
2. Business value achieved
3. Upcoming initiatives

4. Additional support needs
5. Strategic alignment

Let's begin with our key achievements..."

3. Sales Strategy Meeting

"Our focus today is threefold: evaluating our current initiatives, identifying improvement areas, and prioritizing our next steps. Let's align our sales approach with evolving market dynamics and customer needs…

Agenda:

1. Market analysis
   - Industry trends
   - Competitor movements
   - Customer needs evolution
2. Territory planning
3. Account prioritization
4. Resource allocation
5. Success metrics

Our current market position shows..."

4. Sales Training Program

"Given the shifting market dynamics, we're here to strengthen our sales arsenal with powerful tools and winning approaches. Let's elevate our sales expertise to new heights through proven strategies and techniques…

Agenda:

1. Success story analysis
   - Winning strategies
   - Customer engagement methods
   - Negotiation techniques
2. Role-play scenarios
3. Objection handling

4. Solution selling approach
5. Effective closing
6. Action planning

Let's begin by examining our recent wins..."

5. Key Account Strategy Meeting

"Strategic accounts drive our growth trajectory. Let's optimize our approach for maximum value creation. Today we'll craft targeted strategies to transform our key account relationships from service providers to strategic growth partners. Let's design approaches that transform client relationships into powerful growth engines…

Agenda:

1. Account health assessment
    - Current engagement level
    - Growth opportunities
    - Risk factors
2. Relationship mapping
3. Value proposition alignment
4. Account-specific initiatives
5. Resource requirements

Let's start with our top accounts..."

6. Sales Tools and Technology Update

"Our digital arsenal empowers our success, today we'll explore tools that will transform our sales effectiveness and client engagement. Let's embrace these technological advances to enhance our competitive advantage…

Agenda:

1. CRM updates
    - New features

    - Best practices
    - Data quality standards
2. Sales intelligence tools
3. Proposal automation
4. Analytics dashboard
5. Training schedule

Let's explore these new capabilities..."

7. Sales Crisis Management: Major Account Emergency

"We're here to address a critical account challenge and implement recovery strategies. This account situation demands immediate, strategic intervention to protect our partnership. Let's align on swift actions to stabilize this key relationship and protect our position...

Agenda:

1. Situation analysis
    - Client concerns
    - Business impact
    - Relationship status
2. Response strategy
3. Resource mobilization
4. Recovery plan
5. Long-term mitigation

Let's understand what really happened and what will be our next steps ..."

Finance Department Scripts

1. Monthly Budget Review

"Our financial discipline shapes business sustainability, today we'll decode our financial metrics to ensure we're optimizing resource allocation. Let's examine how our financial strategies are supporting business growth and stability...

Agenda:

1. Revenue analysis
   - Department-wise performance
   - Variance analysis
   - Trend identification
2. Expense review
3. Cash flow status
4. Forecast updates
5. Risk mitigation

Starting with our revenue performance..."

2. Investment Committee Meeting

"Capital allocation drives our future. Our focus today is identifying investments that will fuel sustainable growth while maintaining financial prudence. Let's analyse these investment opportunities to maximize returns while managing risk…

Agenda:

1. Project proposals review
   - ROI analysis
   - Risk assessment
   - Implementation timeline
2. Budget allocation
3. Funding options
4. Approval process
5. Monitoring mechanisms

Let's begin with the highest priority proposals..."

3. Stakeholder Financial Review

"Our financial performance story reflects our strategic execution. Today's analysis goes beyond numbers. We're evaluating how our financial strategies are driving business growth and sustainability for our key stakeholders. We'll present a comprehensive view of our financial health and growth trajectory…

Agenda:

1. Financial performance
   - Key metrics
   - Growth indicators
   - Profitability analysis
2. Market conditions
3. Risk management
4. Strategic initiatives
5. Future outlook

Let's start with our key performance indicators..."

4. Tax Planning Session

"Strategic tax planning strengthens our financial foundation, today we'll architect tax strategies that balance compliance with efficiency. Let's align our tax planning with both regulatory requirements and business objectives…

Agenda:

1. Current tax position
   - Tax liabilities
   - Compliance status
   - Filing deadlines
2. Tax optimization opportunities
3. Regulatory changes impact
4. Documentation requirements
5. Risk mitigation

Let's begin with our tax overview..."

5. Financial Systems Update

"Smart resource allocation drives competitive advantage, our goal is to upgrade our financial systems. Let's examine how these technological advances will transform our financial operations...

Agenda:

1. Current system assessment
    - o Pain points
    - o Integration issues
    - o Efficiency gaps
2. Proposed solutions
3. Implementation timeline
4. Training requirements
5. Change management plan

Let's begin reviewing our system landscape by discussing..."

6. Cost Optimization Workshop

"Resource efficiency drives competitive advantage – let's identify opportunities for strategic optimization. Let's design approaches that optimize costs while protecting strategic investments...

Agenda:

1. Cost structure analysis
    - o Fixed vs variable costs
    - o Cost drivers
    - o Benchmark comparison
2. Savings opportunities
3. Implementation approach
4. Impact assessment
5. Monitoring framework

Let's start with our cost breakdown..."

7. Finance Crisis Management: Compliance Issue

"Financial integrity underpins our success. This compliance situation demands immediate attention and strategic resolution. We're here to address a critical compliance matter and implement corrective measures. Let's align on swift actions to manage this compliance challenge effectively...

Agenda:

1. Issue overview
   - Nature of concern
   - Regulatory impact
   - Risk assessment
2. Legal implications
3. Corrective actions
4. Reporting requirements
5. Prevention strategy

Let's begin with the compliance issue..."

Operations Department Scripts

1. Daily Operations Review

"Our operational metrics tell a story of efficiency and challenges. Let's decode these insights to drive improvements.

Agenda:

1. Production metrics
   - Output vs target
   - Quality parameters
   - Resource utilization
2. Bottleneck analysis
3. Safety incidents
4. Maintenance issues
5. Action items

Starting with yesterday's performance..."

2. Process Improvement Meeting

"As we pursue operational excellence, let's examine how we can streamline our processes for maximum impact...

Agenda:

1. Current process analysis
    - Efficiency metrics
    - Pain points
    - Improvement opportunities
2. Proposed solutions
3. Resource requirements
4. Implementation plan
5. Success metrics

Let's begin with our current efficiency data..."

3. Vendor Review Meeting

"I appreciate everyone making time for this important...

Agenda:

1. Performance metrics
    - Delivery compliance
    - Quality standards
    - Cost effectiveness
2. Issue resolution
3. Improvement areas
4. Future requirements
5. Contract terms review

Let's start with the performance dashboard..."

4. Facility Management Review

"Operational infrastructure drives our delivery capability – today we'll focus on optimizing our facility effectiveness. Our discussion centers on aligning our facility capabilities with our growing operational needs…

Agenda:

1. Infrastructure health
   - Equipment status
   - Maintenance schedule
   - Upgrade requirements
2. Safety compliance
3. Energy efficiency
4. Space utilization
5. Budget alignment

Let's begin with infrastructure updates..."

5. Inventory Management Meeting

"Today we'll examine closely how well we are doing inventory management and explore ways to optimize it...

Agenda:

1. Stock level analysis
   - Current inventory
   - Aging report
   - Storage optimization
2. Demand forecasting
3. Supplier performance
4. Cost reduction opportunities
5. Technology integration

Let's review our inventory metrics..."

6. Operational Excellence Workshop

"Today's workshop focuses on balancing operational efficiency with unwavering quality standards. Through lean principles…

Agenda:

1. Current state assessment
   - Process mapping
   - Waste identification
   - Value stream analysis
2. Improvement opportunities
3. Implementation roadmap
4. Resource requirements
5. Success metrics

Let's start with our value stream maps..."

7. Crisis Management: Supply Chain Disruption

"Given the urgent situation, let's get straight to the critical supply chain disruption we're facing.

Agenda:

1. Situation assessment
   - Affected materials/services
   - Impact on production
   - Customer commitments
2. Alternative suppliers
3. Buffer stock utilization
4. Customer communication
5. Recovery timeline

Let's begin with the disruption details..."

Quality Department Scripts

1. Quality Metrics Review

"Our quality metrics reflect our commitment to excellence – let's analyze how we're delivering on this promise. Let's dive into our performance data and identify opportunities to enhance both quality and productivity...

Agenda:

1. Quality metrics
   - Defect rates
   - Customer complaints
   - Process compliance
2. Root cause analysis
3. Corrective actions
4. Preventive measures
5. Training needs

Let's begin with this month's metrics..."

2. Audit Preparation Meeting

"Our audit readiness reflects our quality culture – today we'll assess our preparedness and address any gaps. Let's ensure our quality systems demonstrate robust compliance and continuous improvement...

Agenda:

1. Audit scope review
   - Focus areas
   - Documentation requirements
   - Process verification
2. Previous findings status
3. Risk areas
4. Team responsibilities
5. Timeline planning

Let's start with the audit requirements..."

3. Quality Training Session

"Quality excellence demands shared understanding – today we'll strengthen our quality mindset and capabilities. Our session focuses on building quality consciousness at every level of operation...

Agenda:

1. Quality policy review
2. Standard operating procedures
3. Common issues and solutions
4. Best practices
5. Assessment criteria

Let's begin with the quality fundamentals..."

4. Supplier Quality Assessment

"Quality excellence begins with our suppliers, today we'll evaluate their performance and partnership potential. Our focus is on strengthening supplier quality to ensure end-to-end excellence in our value chain…

Agenda:

1. Supplier ratings
    - Quality metrics
    - Compliance status
    - Improvement trends
2. Audit findings
3. Corrective actions
4. Development plans
5. Resource allocation

Let's review our supplier performance..."

5. Product Quality Review

"Our discussion centres on assessing our product quality through some specific parameters.

Agenda:

1. Quality metrics analysis
    - Defect rates
    - Customer feedback
    - Field performance

2. Enhancement opportunities
3. Testing protocols
4. Documentation updates
5. Training needs

Let's examine our product quality indicators..."

6. Quality Management System Update

"Let's methodically review our quality management system to ensure we're showcasing operational excellence...

Agenda:

1. System changes
    - New requirements
    - Process updates
    - Documentation revisions
2. Implementation timeline
3. Training schedule
4. Validation process
5. Compliance monitoring

We will begin to review the system updates..."

7. Crisis Management: Quality Incident Response

"This emergency meeting addresses the critical quality incident reported.

Agenda:

1. Incident overview
    - Affected products
    - Customer impact
    - Risk assessment
2. Containment actions
3. Root cause analysis

4. Corrective measures
5. Stakeholder communication

Let's begin with the incident details and then we will examine recent quality challenges to enhance our prevention strategies. "

Delivery Team Scripts

1. Project Status Review

"As we evaluate our project landscape, let's focus on identifying both successes and areas needing intervention. Today we'll assess where we stand and what lies ahead...

Agenda:

1. Project metrics
   - Timeline adherence
   - Resource utilization
   - Quality parameters
   - Client satisfaction
2. Risk assessment
3. Resource allocation
4. Client communications
5. Next week's priorities

Let's start with our critical projects..."

2. Client Delivery Review

"Our commitment to client success drives today's discussion on delivery milestones and value creation. Let's examine how our delivery strategies are meeting and exceeding client expectations...

Agenda:

1. Deliverable status
   - Completed items
   - Upcoming milestones
   - Quality metrics

2. Issue resolution
3. Change requests
4. Resource planning
5. Success stories

Let's begin with our key achievements..."

3. Team Capacity Planning

"Resource optimization is crucial for delivery excellence. Let's align our capacity with upcoming commitments. Today we'll map our talent deployment to ensure seamless project execution. Our focus is on building a robust resource plan that balances team capabilities with project demands…

Agenda:

1. Project pipeline
   - Confirmed projects
   - Potential projects
   - Resource requirements
2. Skill matrix review
3. Training needs
4. Risk mitigation
5. Timeline planning

Let's start with our project forecast..."

4. Sprint Retrospective

"Let's candidly discuss our sprint journey, celebrating successes and learning from challenges. Today's retrospective will help us fine-tune our delivery approach for greater agility and impact.

Agenda:

1. Sprint performance
   - Completed stories

   - Velocity metrics
   - Quality indicators
2. Team feedback
3. Process improvements
4. Action items
5. Next sprint planning

Let's begin with our achievements..."

5. Release Planning Meeting

"Our upcoming release demands precision planning. Let's ensure we're set up for flawless execution. Today we'll orchestrate our release strategy to minimize risks and maximize value delivery.

Agenda:

1. Feature scope
   - Core functionalities
   - Dependencies
   - Integration points
2. Resource allocation
3. Timeline planning
4. Risk assessment
5. Communication strategy Let's review the release scope..."

6. Stakeholder Alignment Meeting

"Successful delivery hinges on stakeholder alignment. Let's ensure we're unified in our approach. Today's meeting focuses on synchronizing expectations and commitments across all stakeholders.

Agenda:

1. Project vision
   - Business objectives
   - Success criteria
   - Value proposition

2. Timeline review
3. Resource commitments
4. Risk management
5. Communication plan Let's align on our project goals..."

7. Crisis Management: Production Issue Response

"Our priority is addressing the production issue impacting our delivery. Let's align on swift action. Given the urgent situation, we'll get straight to...

Agenda:

1. Issue assessment
   - o System impact
   - o User impact
   - o Business impact
2. Root cause analysis
3. Resolution options
4. Implementation plan
5. Customer communication

Let's begin with the situation overview..."

IT/Technology Department Scripts

1. IT Team Review Meeting

"Today we'll evaluate how our IT capabilities are enabling business success and innovation. Let's examine our technology metrics and align our priorities to drive organizational agility…

Agenda:

1. Service metrics review
   - o System uptime
   - o Incident response times
   - o Ticket resolution rates
   - o Customer satisfaction scores

2. Project status updates
3. Resource allocation
4. Training needs
5. Process improvements

Let's begin with our service metrics..."

2. Technology Strategic Planning

"Today's session will shape our technology roadmap to drive competitive advantage and innovation. Let's envision and plan the next generation of our technology landscape and digital capabilities...

Agenda:

1. Current landscape assessment
   - Infrastructure status
   - Application portfolio
   - Technical debt
   - Security posture
2. Future state vision
3. Gap analysis
4. Investment priorities
5. Implementation timeline Let's start with our current state..."

3. Digital Transformation Initiative Launch

"Today marks the beginning of our digital evolution, one that will redefine how we create value. As we launch this digital transformation initiative, let's align on our vision for technological excellence...

Agenda:

1. Program overview
   - Vision and objectives
   - Key initiatives
   - Success metrics

2. Implementation approach
3. Change management
4. Resource requirements
5. Risk mitigation

Let's explore our transformation journey..."

4. IT Security Review

"In today's threat landscape, our security posture demands continuous scrutiny and enhancement. Today's focus is on evaluating and elevating our security measures to protect our digital assets…

Agenda:

1. Security assessment
   - o Threat landscape
   - o Vulnerability status
   - o Compliance requirements
2. Security initiatives
3. Training programs
4. Incident response
5. Budget allocation

Let's begin with reviewing our security metrics..."

5. Crisis Management: Security Breach Response

"Given the security incident at hand, let's prioritize tackling this pressing issue...

Agenda:

1. Incident assessment
   - o Nature of breach
   - o Systems affected
   - o Data exposure risk

2. Containment measures
3. Investigation status
4. Communication plan
5. Recovery steps

Let's begin with understanding what was the breach..."

Marketing Department Scripts

1. Marketing Team Review

"Today we'll analyse how our marketing strategies are shaping customer perceptions and driving engagement. Let's examine our marketing metrics and align our efforts for maximum market impact...

Agenda:

1. Campaign performance
    - o Digital metrics
    - o Lead generation
    - o Conversion rates
    - o ROI analysis
2. Content calendar
3. Budget utilization
4. Upcoming initiatives
5. Resource planning

We will start with our campaign metrics..."

2. Brand Strategy Session

"As custodians of our brand, we're here to resonate more powerfully with our evolving market. Today we'll craft strategies to elevate our brand presence and deepen customer connections...

Agenda:

1. Market analysis
    - o Brand perception

    - Competitor positioning
    - Customer insights
2. Brand evolution
3. Communication strategy
4. Channel optimization
5. Success metrics

Let's begin with market insights..."

3. Campaign Launch Planning

"Today we'll architect a campaign strategy that breaks through the noise and delivers impact. Let's design a campaign that not only reaches our audience but inspires action and builds loyalty…

Agenda:

1. Campaign overview
    - Objectives
    - Target audience
    - Key messages
  - Channel strategy
2. Creative concepts
3. Timeline planning
4. Budget allocation
5. Success metrics

Let's start with reviewing the campaign brief..."

4. Marketing Performance Review

"Our metrics tell the story of our market impact – let's decode these insights to drive future success…

Agenda:

1. Performance metrics
    - Channel performance

    - Campaign results
    - Lead quality
    - Market share
2. ROI analysis
3. Strategy alignment
4. Resource optimization
5. Future priorities

Let's examine our performance data..."

5. Crisis Management: Brand Issue Response

"Given the current brand situation, we need swift, strategic action to protect our market position. Our priority is addressing this brand challenge while maintaining stakeholder confidence...

Agenda:

1. Situation analysis
    - Issue description
    - Public perception
    - Brand impact
2. Response strategy
3. Media management
4. Stakeholder communication
5. Recovery plan

Let's assess the situation firstly..."

R&D Team Scripts

1. Research Team Review

"Today we'll examine our research progress and ensure we're pushing the boundaries of innovation. Let's assess how our research endeavours are advancing our technological leadership...

Agenda:

1. Project status
   - Active research
   - Preliminary findings
   - Resource utilization
   - Timeline adherence
2. Innovation pipeline
3. Publication status
4. Collaboration updates
5. Resource needs

Let's begin with active projects..."

2. Innovation Strategy Meeting

"Today we'll architect our innovation roadmap to maintain our competitive edge and market leadership. Let's align our innovation strategy with emerging opportunities and technological frontier…

Agenda:

1. Market trends
   - Technology advances
   - Customer needs
   - Competitive landscape
2. Research priorities
3. Resource allocation
4. Partnership opportunities
5. Success metrics

Let's start with market insights..."

3. New Research Project Launch

"Today marks the beginning of a crucial research initiative that could redefine our industry. As we launch this groundbreaking project, let's align on our vision and execution approach…

Agenda:

1. Project overview
   - Research objectives
   - Methodology
   - Expected outcomes
2. Team structure
3. Resource allocation
4. Timeline planning
5. Risk management

Let's explore the project scope..."

4. Research Portfolio Review

"Today we'll evaluate our research investments and ensure they align with our strategic vision. Let's examine how our research portfolio is driving competitive advantage and future growth...

Agenda:

1. Portfolio analysis
   - Project mix
   - Resource allocation
   - Success rates
   - Value generation
2. Pipeline health
3. Resource optimization
4. Strategic alignment
5. Future priorities

Let's examine our success metrics..."

5. Crisis Management: Research Setback

"In research, challenges often lead to breakthroughs, let's address this setback strategically. Today we'll tackle our research challenge head-on and identify alternative pathways...

Agenda:

1. Issue assessment
    - Technical challenges
    - Timeline impact
    - Resource implications
2. Alternative approaches
3. Recovery plan
4. Stakeholder communication
5. Risk mitigation

Let's review the situation..."

Legal/Compliance Department Scripts

1. Legal Team Review

"As guardians of corporate governance, we must balance protection with progression. Today we'll evaluate our legal landscape and ensure our strategies protect and advance our business objectives. Let's examine our legal portfolio and align our resources with emerging challenges and opportunities…

Agenda:

1. Case status review
    - Active litigation
    - Regulatory matters
    - Contract reviews
    - Compliance issues
2. Resource allocation
3. Budget status
4. Training needs
5. Process improvements

Let's start with the active cases..."

2. Compliance Strategy Planning

"As stewards of corporate integrity, we're here to strengthen our compliance framework. Let's design a robust compliance roadmap that anticipates regulatory evolution and business needs...

Agenda:

1. Regulatory landscape
   - New requirements
   - Upcoming changes
   - Impact assessment
2. Implementation plan
3. Resource needs
4. Training program
5. Monitoring framework

Let's begin by reviewing the regulatory requirements..."

3. Compliance Program Launch

"We're launching a compliance initiative that will set new standards for organizational excellence. Let's roll out a compliance program that embeds best practices into our organizational DNA...

Agenda:

1. Program overview
   - Objectives
   - Key components
   - Implementation approach
2. Timeline planning
3. Resource allocation
4. Training schedule
5. Success metrics

Let's examine the program structure..."

4. Legal Risk Assessment

"Proactive risk management demands rigorous analysis, let's assess our risk portfolio and strengthen our preventive measures…

Agenda:

1. Risk analysis
    - Litigation exposure
    - Regulatory compliance
    - Contract risks
    - IP protection
2. Mitigation strategies
3. Resource requirements
4. Action planning
5. Monitoring framework

Let's begin with the risk assessment..."

5. Crisis Management: Legal Emergency

"We're here to address a critical legal challenge and determine our response strategy. Let's align on swift, decisive actions to manage this legal situation effectively…

Agenda:

1. Situation overview
    - Legal implications
    - Business impact
    - Stakeholder concerns
2. Response strategy
3. Resource mobilization
4. Communication plan
5. Risk mitigation

Let's assess the situation first..."

Appendices: Reference Repository

Appendix A: Power Scripts for Interview Success

Opening: "Tell Me About Yourself"

The Story Arc Formula
I've spent [X] years in [industry], specializing in [key skill]. At [current/recent company], I led [specific achievement] that resulted in [measurable impact]. I'm now looking to [future goal] where I can apply my expertise in [relevant skills] to drive similar results.

Industry-Specific Examples
Tech: *My journey in software development started at [Company], where I led a team that reduced deployment time by 60%. Currently at [Company], I'm architecting cloud solutions that have cut infrastructure costs by 40%. I'm eager to bring this experience to help scale your platform."*

Sales: *I began my sales career at [Company], consistently exceeding quota by 130%. At [Current Company], I've built a team that's grown revenue from $2M to $8M in 18 months. I'm excited about the opportunity to replicate this success in your expanding market.*

Handling Tough Questions

Weakness Question
I've learned that my attention to detail, while a strength, can sometimes impact speed. I've addressed this by implementing a '2-minute rule' - if a review takes longer, I schedule it separately. This has improved my productivity while maintaining quality.

Gap in Employment

I used that time to [upskill/certification/project], which led to [specific outcome]. This focused period helped me clarify my career goals and confirm that [role/industry] is where I can add the most value.

Why Leave Current Role?

While I've gained valuable experience leading [achievement], I'm looking for opportunities to [specific growth area] that align with [company's mission/project]. Your role offers exactly that challenge.

Salary Expectations

Based on my experience [specific achievements] and market research, I'm targeting [range] for this role. I'm flexible and open to discussion based on the total package.

Smart Questions to Ask

About the Role: *What would success look like in the first 6 months of this role?" "How does this role contribute to the company's major initiatives for this year?*

About Growth: *How has this team evolved over the past year, and what's your vision for its future?" "What development opportunities are available for top performers?*

About Culture: *Can you share an example of how the team has col- laborated to overcome a recent challenge? What qualities define your most successful employees?*

Closing Statements

The Interest Closer

This conversation has reinforced my excitement about [specific aspect of role/company]. My experience in [relevant achievement] aligns perfectly with your needs in [mentioned challenge], and I'm confident I can deliver similar results here.

The Value Closer

Based on our discussion about [key challenge mentioned], I see a clear opportunity to apply my experience in [relevant skill] to help achieve [specific goal]. I'm excited about the possibility of contributing to your team's success.

The Follow-Up Closer

Thank you for sharing such detailed insights about [specific discussion point]. This role aligns perfectly with my goals in [area], and I'm very interested in moving forward. What are the next steps in your process?

Power Phrases for Any Moment

Handling Uncertainty

While I haven't encountered that specific situation, my experience handling [similar challenge] has taught me that...

Demonstrating Leadership

I saw an opportunity to improve [process], took initiative to [action], which resulted in [measurable outcome].

Showing Growth

That experience taught me the importance of [lesson], which I've since applied to [new situation] with great success.

Remember: Sincerity speaks louder than scripted responses. Use these scripts as frameworks, not rigid answers, and adapt them to reflect your genuine experience and style.

Appendix B: Enhancing Your Industry Vocabulary

Technology & Digital

- The new mobile app reduced customer service calls by X% in the first month.
- Moving to cloud storage cut our monthly costs while doubling storage capacity.
- Weekly product updates have increased user engagement across all age groups.
- Automated customer onboarding now handles X new signups daily without delays.
- Enhanced security protocols blocked over X potential threats last quarter.

Finance & Banking

- Digital payment adoption surged, significantly reducing cash transactions.
- AI-driven fraud detection prevented substantial financial losses.
- Our new investment portfolio outperformed market returns.
- Streamlined loan approvals cut waiting times drastically.
- Customer-centric financial planning services improved client retention.

Marketing & Advertising

- Data-driven campaigns led to a massive increase in customer engagement.
- Influencer partnerships expanded brand reach significantly.
- Video content became the dominant driver of social media interactions.

- A/B testing greatly improved email click-through rates.
- Behavioral analytics provided deep customer insights, refining messaging strategies.

Retail & E-Commerce

- Personalized marketing campaigns boosted average order value.
- AI-powered chatbots resolved the majority of customer queries without human intervention.
- Faster supply chain logistics significantly reduced delivery times.
- Subscription-based services drove a major increase in recurring revenue.

Manufacturing & Supply Chain

- Lean manufacturing processes reduced production waste.
- Predictive maintenance significantly cut machine downtime.
- Sustainable sourcing strategies lowered costs and enhanced ESG compliance.
- Robotics and automation accelerated assembly line efficiency.
- Real-time inventory tracking minimized stock shortages and surplus.

Healthcare & Pharmaceuticals

- AI-assisted diagnostics enhanced early disease detection.
- Our tele-medicine platform now connects thousands of patients with specialists monthly.
- The latest drug formulation reduced treatment duration.
- Hospital automation improved efficiency and reduced patient check-in time.
- Preventive care programs led to a noticeable drop in hospitalization rates

Energy and Sustainability

- Smart grids optimized electricity distribution, reducing waste.
- Renewable energy initiatives led to a significant drop in carbon emissions.
- Green building initiatives lowered operational costs.
- Waste-to-energy solutions now power thousands of homes.
- Electric vehicle adoption programs cut fuel dependence dramatically.

Appendix C:
Strategic Idioms for Business Success

Financial Idioms

- Break even- Neither profit nor loss
- Cash cow- Consistent profit generator
- Tighten our belts - Reduce spending
- Bottom line - Final total or result
- Deep pockets - Having substantial financial resources
- Burn through cash - To spend money quickly and perhaps wastefully
- Cook the books - Manipulate financial records illegally

Examples:

- *Our new software product has become a real cash cow for the company.*
- *We need to tighten our belts this quarter to improve our bottom line.*
- *The startup finally broke even after two years of operation.*
- *We need an investor with deep pockets to fund this expansion phase.*
- *The startup is burning through cash with their aggressive expansion strategy.*
- *Let's crunch the numbers and come up with a ball park figure for next year's budget.*

Management and Leadership Idioms

- Climb the corporate ladder - Advance in one's career
- Bite the bullet - Make a difficult decision
- Wear many hats - Perform multiple roles
- Call the shots - Make important decisions
- Across the board - Including everyone or everything
- Run a tight ship - To manage an organization strictly and efficiently

Examples:

- *As a startup founder, you often have to wear many hats.*
- *Let's not put all our eggs in one basket; we should diversify our investments.*
- *In this crisis, we need a leader who can call the shots decisively.*
- *Under the new COO, we're running a tight ship with strict performance metrics.*

Project and Task-Related Idioms

- Burn the midnight oil - Work late hours
- Hit the ground running - Start quickly and efficiently
- All in a day's work – A task that falls into normal daily work routines
- Cut corners - Do something in the easiest or cheapest way
- Reinvent the wheel - Waste time doing something that's already been done
- Crunch time - A critical period of intense pressure
- Iron out the kinks - To resolve minor problems or difficulties
- Bite off more than you can chew - To take on more responsibility than you can handle

Examples:

- *The project failed, so it's back to the drawing board for our team.*
- *Dealing with emergencies is all in a day's work*
- *Don't cut corners on quality control; it'll cost us more in the long run.*
- *There's no need to reinvent the wheel; let's use the existing template.*
- *Once we iron out the kinks in the new software, it should run smoothly.*
- *Let's dive into the nitty-gritties of the new software system!*

Communication Idioms

- Touch base - Brief communication
- Keep in the loop - Keep informed
- On the same page - In agreement
- Get the message across - Communicate effectively
- Read between the lines - Understand hidden meanings
- Give someone a heads up - Inform in advance
- Put it on the radar - To bring attention to something that needs consideration

Examples:

- *Let's touch base next week to discuss the project progress.*
- *Please keep me in the loop regarding any changes to the client's requirements.*
- *I'll give you a heads up before the big announcement.*
- *You've been knocking it out of the park with your recent projects; keep up the good work.*
- *I'm putting it on the radar that our main competitor is planning to enter our market next quarter.*

Market and Competition Idioms

- Corner the market - Dominate a market segment
- Raise the bar - Set higher standards
- Level playing field - Fair competition
- Cut-throat competition - Intense, fierce competition
- Get a piece of the pie - Obtain a share of the profits

Examples:

- *Our new product line has really helped us corner the market in sustainable packaging.*
- *The new regulations aim to create a level playing field for all competitors.*

- *With this innovative feature, we're raising the bar for the entire industry.*
- *Our team is working around the clock to bring you the best products and services.*
- *Our commitment to delivering exceptional products and services is unwavering.*

Problem-Solving Idioms

- Piece of cake - Easy task
- Put out fires - Deal with urgent problems
- Bite off more than you can chew - Take on too much
- Go back to square one - Start over from the beginning
- Bang your head against the wall - To try to solve a problem with no success

Examples:

- *The IT department is constantly putting out fires due to the outdated system.*
- *We've been banging our heads against the wall trying to fix this technical issue.*
- *The support team spent all week putting out fires caused by the system upgrade.*

Time and Deadline Idioms

- Down to the wire - Last minute
- In crunch time - Critical period with pressure
- Race against time - To work quickly to meet a deadline
- Eleventh hour - The last possible moment
- Beat the clock - Finish before a deadline
- Around the clock - All day and night
- Eleventh hour - Very late in a process

Examples:

- *We're down to the wire on this project, so everyone needs to focus.*
- *The team worked around the clock to deliver the proposal on time.*
- *We're racing against time to prepare the pitch deck for tomorrow's investor meeting*
- *Even at the eleventh hour, we were still making changes to the presentation.*

Team and Collaboration Idioms

- Pull your weight - Contribute fairly
- On board - Agree or participate
- Team player - Collaborative individual
- Get your ducks in a row - Organize and prepare thoroughly
- On the same wavelength - Think in a similar way
- Play devil's advocate - To present a counter-argument for the sake of debate
- Get everyone on board - To gain support from all participant
- Bring to the table - Contribute skills or resources

Examples:

- *We need everyone to pull their weight to meet this deadline.*
- *Let's get our ducks in a row before the client meeting tomorrow.*
- *What unique skills do you bring to the table for this project?*
- *Let me play devil's advocate - what if the market reacts negatively to this pricing strategy?*
- *Before launching the initiative, we need to get everyone on board with the new procedures.*

Success and Failure Idioms

- Hit the jackpot - Great success
- Miss the boat - Miss an opportunity

- Go through the roof - Increase dramatically
- Fall flat - Fail to achieve the desired impact
- Knock it out of the park - To be extremely successful
- Hit the nail on the head - Do or say exactly the right thing

Examples:

- *Our sales have gone through the roof since we launched the new marketing campaign.*
- *Our Q4 sales team knocked it out of the park with 200% of their target.*
- *If we don't act now, we might miss the boat on this emerging market trend.*
- *We missed the boat on cloud computing and now we're playing catch-up with competitors.*
- *The new product launch fell flat due to poor market research.*

Appendix D: Diplomatic Communication Scripts for Workplace Scenarios

Scenario 1: Delivering Constructive Feedback

"I'd like to discuss some recent projects with you. I value your contributions to our team, which is why I want to share something I've noticed. The quality we're known for seems to be slipping in recent deliverables. Specifically, I noticed inconsistent formatting and data discrepancies in the latest client presentation."

"I appreciate your openness about feeling overwhelmed. Let's work together to find a balance between speed and quality. What would help you manage these competing demands better?"

"I like your suggestion about review time. Would it help if we set up a peer review system? We could partner you with a colleague for quick quality checks before final submissions."

"Let's implement this for two weeks and then meet again to assess how it's working. I'll also review your current workload to ensure it's manageable. How does this plan sound?"

Scenario 2: Addressing Performance Issues

"Thank you for making time today. I've noticed some recent changes in your project delivery, especially with the Wilson account. I'd like to understand your perspective on what's happening."

"I hear how challenging these shifting client requirements are. Let's figure out how to handle this together. What kind of support would be most helpful right now?"

"A change request protocol could help set clearer boundaries and manage client expectations while protecting your workflow. I can draft this by Friday for your review, and I'm happy to join your next client call to help establish these parameters."

Scenario 3: Mediating Team Conflicts

"Thank you both for being here. I've observed some tension around project ownership, and I believe we need to address this openly. I'd like to hear both perspectives so we can find a constructive path forward."

"I want to acknowledge both viewpoints here. One side needs recognition and inclusion in the implementation process, while the other prioritizes efficient execution and meeting deadlines. Let's find a way to achieve both."

"I suggest we implement daily 15-minute alignment meetings to discuss changes and ensure everyone's contributions are recognized. We can test this for two weeks and adjust as needed."

"Remember, your different approaches - thoughtful input and efficient execution - actually complement each other. When we balance these strengths, it benefits the entire project."

Scenario 4: Addressing Remote Work Productivity Concerns

"I wanted to connect about some observations regarding our remote work arrangement. While I appreciate your consistent meeting attendance, I've noticed some delays in project updates and response times to team communications."

"I understand that working remotely can present unique challenges with visibility and coordination. Could you help me understand what obstacles you're experiencing in your current setup?"

"Let's try these adjustments for the next two weeks and then reassess. I'm committed to helping you succeed in this remote environment while maintaining our team's effectiveness. How does this approach sound to you?"

Appendix E: Executive Communication Strategies for Different Groups

This section covers various examples for engaging with key stakeholder groups, ensuring that each receives the information they need, in the way they prefer to receive it, when they need it most.

Board and Investors:

- **Focus on strategic direction and value creation**
  Quarterly board presentation on "Strategic Growth Initiatives" showing clear links between investments and projected ROI: "Our $10M digital transformation initiative is projected to reduce operational costs by 25% within 18 months"
- **Regular updates on key metrics and milestones**
  Weekly dashboard showing critical KPIs: revenue growth, customer acquisition costs, churn rates, and pipeline health with year-over-year comparisons
- **Clear articulation of challenges and opportunities**
  While facing supply chain disruptions in Asia (estimated impact: $2M), we've identified alternate suppliers that could reduce costs by 15% long-term
- **Proactive risk communication**
  Cybersecurity audit revealed three medium-risk vulnerabilities; remediation plan attached with 30-day completion timeline

Employees:

- **Regular town halls and team meetings**
  Weekly department standups with rotating focus areas: technical updates, customer feedback, process improvements
- **Transparent sharing of company direction**
  We invested heavily in R&D this quarter, here's why and what it means for our future

- **Open door policy for concerns**
  "Leadership Office Hours" where employees can book 15-minute slots with any executive to discuss concerns
- **Recognition and celebration of achievements**
  Quarterly achievement ceremonies recognizing both individual and team contributions to company goals

Customers and Partners:

- **Regular business reviews**
  We've maintained X% uptime and resolved Y% of tickets within Z hours.
- **Product/service roadmap sharing**
  Here's what's coming in the next X months and how it addresses your specific needs.
- **Feedback incorporation**
  Customer advisory board meetings where top clients help prioritize development roadmap.
- **Joint planning sessions**
  Let's map our technology roadmap to your business objectives for the next year.

Community and Regulators:

- **Proactive engagement on key issues**
  Our expansion plans will create 200 local jobs; let's discuss how to maximize community benefit.
- **Regular reporting and updates**
  Monthly compliance dashboards showing key regulatory metrics with trend analysis
- **Participation in community initiatives**
  Our engineers mentor 50 high school students annually.
- **Compliance and transparency in reporting**
  Real-time emissions monitoring dashboard available to regulatory bodies and the public

Epilogue

Strategies for Lifelong Learning and Improvement

As we conclude this journey through business communication, remember that mastery is not a destination but a continuous path of growth. Each email you craft, presentation you deliver, and conversa- tion you lead is an opportunity to refine your skills.

The most effective communicators share one common trait: they never stop learning. They view every interaction as a chance to experiment with new approaches, gather feedback, and adapt their style. They record their presentations to study their delivery, seek honest feedback from trusted colleagues, and regularly step out of their comfort zones.

Consider starting small. Pick one aspect of your communication to focus on each week. Perhaps it's improving your storytelling, mastering data presentation, or enhancing your listening skills.

Remember that perfection isn't the goal but the progress is. As you move forward, stay curious. Observe how others communicate effectively. Study their techniques. But most importantly, develop your authentic voice. Your unique perspective and experiences are valuable assets in your communication journey.

The tools and strategies in this book are just the beginning. Your real growth will come from applying them, learning from both successes and setbacks, and consistently pushing yourself to become a more effective communicator.

In the end, strategic communication is about creating impact that resonates long after you leave the room.

Acknowledgements

This book was shaped by many hands and hearts. I am deeply grateful to each person who played a role to bringing this vision to life.

My deepest gratitude to Harjeet Khanduja for crafting an inspiring foreword that beautifully captures the essence of this book's mission.

To my daughter Alaina, whose keen eye and thoughtful suggestions transformed these pages. Her insights brought clarity and precision to my words. To my family and extended family, your unwavering love and support gave me the strength to keep writing. Your belief in me made this possible.

Special thanks to the thoughtful reviewers who whose valuable insights and candid feedback elevated this work.

To my teachers, mentors, friends, well-wishers, and clients - each of you has imparted invaluable lessons at just the right moments. This book carries the wisdom of our shared experiences.

And to my beloved husband - my rock and my greatest cheerleader–thank you for always pushing me beyond my comfort zone and encouraging me to strive for excellence.

And my heartfelt thanks To you, dear reader, thank you for embarking on this path with me.

Finally, my deepest gratitude to the Almighty for guiding me toward this purpose. May this work serve as a meaningful contribution for many lives in the times to come.

About the Author

Preeti Subberwal is an accomplished Executive Presence Coach and a Leadership Trainer with over 22 years of corporate experience, including more than a decade in IT. She is on a mission to help professionals unlock their leadership X-factor by harnessing both their inner radiance and outer brilliance.

Preeti has impacted people from 150+ companies across 40+ industries, including global giants like PwC, Infosys, KPMG, BMW, Salesforce, Accenture, Cisco, DELL, Deloitte, Sanofi, Vivo, Emaar, CSIR, Tata, and Hero Group.

She specializes in elevating executive and leadership presence, helping professionals enhance their strategic influence, communication skills, public speaking and stage presence.

Who can Benefit from Preeti's Expertise?

- **Aspiring Leaders**: Professionals seeking to inspire action and ignite team performance
- **Business Owners**: Entrepreneurs aiming to establish themselves as domain experts and attract high-value clients
- **Career Professionals**: Individuals preparing for promotions or crucial interviews
- **Entrepreneurs**: Those looking to reinvent their professional image and brand

Partner with Preeti to maximize your executive impact and exercise strategic influence in your professional journey.

For coaching and collaboration inquiries, reach out at:
Email: preeti.subberwal@gmail.com
Website: www.preetisubberwal.com